MISSION TO PLUTO

clarionbooks.com

Book design by Yay! Design
The illustrations in this book were created digitally in Illustrator.
The text type was set in Gill Sans.
The display type was set in Handel Gothic.

The Library of Congress has cataloged the hardcover edition as follows:
Names: Carson, Mary Kay, author. | Uhlman, Tom, illustrator.
Title: Mission to Pluto : the first visit to an ice dwarf and the Kuiper belt /
Mary Kay Carson ; with photographs by Tom Uhlman.
Other titles: Scientists in the field.
Description: Boston : Houghton Mifflin Harcourt, [2016] | Series: Scientists
in the field | Audience: Ages 10–12.– | Audience: Grades 4 to 6.–
Identifiers: LCCN 2015037656
Subjects: LCSH: New Horizons (Spacecraft)—Juvenile literature. | Space
flight—Juvenile literature. | Interplanetary voyages—Juvenile
literature. | Pluto (Dwarf planet)—Juvenile literature. | Kuiper
Belt—Juvenile literature. | Outer space—Exploration—Juvenile literature.
Classification: LCC QB701 .C37 2016 | DDC 629.43/54922—dc23
LC record available at http://lccn.loc.gov/2015037656

ISBN: 978-0-544-41671-0 hardcover
ISBN: 978-0-358-24027-3 paperback

Manufactured in China
SCP 10 9 8 7 6 5 4 3 2
4500837616

Mary Kay Carson

with photographs by Tom Uhlman

MISSION TO PLUTO

The First Visit to an Ice Dwarf and the Kuiper Belt

Clarion Books

An Imprint of HarperCollins*Publishers*

Boston   New York

For our space enthusiast nephew, Noah George Basso —M.K.C. and T.U.

CONTENTS

ONE

A LONG-AWAITED ENCOUNTER

The large meeting room was packed and noisy.
Hundreds of people mingled, holding small American flags, chatting with excitement, and eating snacks. Some wore black shirts with an official nine-sided mission patch that showed a small robotic spacecraft flying above a peach-colored dwarf planet with a moon in the background. The crowd also included family members, guests from across the globe, television crews, reporters, and even a few celebrities such as Bill Nye, the Science Guy.

At the front of the room, the grown children of astronomer Clyde Tombaugh spoke to the audience. The dozens of big-screen televisions throughout the room, lobby, and huge overflow tent outside mirrored their proud smiling faces. "When my dad discovered Pluto, he only saw a speck of light," seventy-five-year-old Annette Tombaugh said. "Now we're finally going to find out what it really

THE CROWD GOES WILD
AS *NEW HORIZONS*
FLIES THROUGH THE
PLUTO SYSTEM.

AMONG THE HONORED GUESTS AT THE FLYBY CELEBRATION WERE ANNETTE AND ALDEN TOMBAUGH, THE PLUTO DISCOVERER CLYDE TOMBAUGH'S DAUGHTER AND SON.

looks like," she told the crowd. Cheers rose from below the stage.

The television screens showed countdown clocks ticking away the seconds, giving the gathering a New Year's Eve party feel; except it was 7:45 in the morning. Cups were filled with coffee, not champagne. By the time the clocks ticked down to less than five minutes, it was standing room only. Onscreen alongside the countdown was a computer image of a busy spacecraft. Its instruments took turns scanning a bright, round space object. And that faraway world was getting closer by the second.

The spacecraft was *New Horizons,* and Pluto its destination.

The crowd began counting down. "Nine, eight, seven, six. . . ." At zero, whoops and cheers rang out. People waved their flags and clapped, and someone with a microphone yelled, "*New Horizons* at Pluto 2015!" More than one face shone with tears. It was a historic moment, after all. The fastest spacecraft ever to leave Earth had just completed the farthest voyage to a target destination and become the first ever to explore Pluto. The small robotic probe on the computer screen didn't pause during all the hoopla. After traveling 3 billion miles (4.8 billion

hard to imagine getting to Pluto without Alan Stern.

Exploring Pluto has been Alan Stern's dream for most of his working life. "Two of my three favorite *p*-words are *patience* and *persistence*," said Alan with a smile. Both were required to get to his other favorite *p*-word, which you can probably guess. (Yep, it's *Pluto*.) His years of effort could be counted in decades. Alan started pushing for a Pluto mission nearly thirty years ago. How does it feel to finally get there? "It feels good, really good," he said.

Alan Stern was a moon-landing kid. He grew up during

"*NEW HORIZONS* IS SOMETHING OUR GRANDKIDS WILL KNOW ABOUT," SAID ALAN. "IT'S A ONCE-IN-A-LIFETIME EXPERIENCE FOR ALL THE ENGINEERS AND SCIENTISTS WHO MAKE UP THE INCREDIBLE NEW HORIZONS TEAM."

kilometers) for nine and a half years, its focus was Pluto. Only 7,750 miles (12,472 kilometers) separated it from the icy surface, about the distance between New York City and Mumbai, India. This was prime time for taking measurements, scanning the surface, and snapping close-up photos. *New Horizons* was flying its closest pass by Pluto. It had work to do.

PATIENCE + PERSISTENCE = PLUTO

"It's a moment of celebration," said a man in a black shirt sporting a mission patch. As the mission's principal investigator, Alan Stern is the leader of the team that designed, built, and flew the spacecraft to Pluto. "The New Horizons team is proud to have accomplished the first exploration of the Pluto system. This mission has inspired people across the world with the excitement of exploration and what humankind can achieve." It's the 1960s–70s while NASA was sending people to the moon. The Apollo astronauts were the first humans to set foot on a space object, the first to walk on another world. The adventure of exploring space was infectious in those days. "Everybody had an astronaut helmet and a little silver Halloween suit," Alan recalled. He caught the astronaut bug early on. "I wanted to be a scientist when I was a little kid," he said. "And I wanted to be an astronaut." Alan studied physics and astronomy in college and earned degrees in aerospace engineering. He also applied for NASA's astronaut program. "I came quite close," he said. "But I wasn't selected in the end."

Alan did work on space missions, though. He helped build astronomy instruments that flew onboard the space shuttles. The *Challenger* disaster of 1986 changed all that. The space shuttle broke apart seventy-three seconds after the launch, killing all seven crew members onboard. Alan knew most of them well. "It was a very personal tragedy," he said. "It was a very difficult period in my life and my career." NASA grounded the entire shuttle fleet for nearly three years after the accident, and Alan decided to make a career change. Designing and building scientific instruments was engineering work. He liked it, but the part that thrilled him the most was studying the findings and

ALAN STERN MIGHT NOT HAVE BECOME A NASA ASTRONAUT, BUT HE STILL PLANS TO FLY INTO SPACE. HE'S BEEN TRAINING FOR A COMMERCIAL SPACE FLIGHT ON VIRGIN'S *GALACTIC*.

THESE COMPUTER-PROCESSED VIEWS OF PLUTO WERE CREATED FROM IMAGES TAKEN BY THE HUBBLE SPACE TELESCOPE; THEY REPRESENTED SCIENTISTS' BEST GUESS FOR WHAT PLUTO LOOKED LIKE BEFORE *NEW HORIZONS* FLEW BY.

90°   180°   270°

making discoveries—the science. "It really swept me off my feet," he said. "I decided I wanted to be a space scientist as a result."

HEAD PLUTO FAN

Studying to be a planetary scientist is how Pluto entered Alan Stern's life. He researched Pluto's atmosphere as a project in college. "I got interested in Pluto because it was such a great unknown." In the 1980s no one knew much about what was then the ninth planet. "It was truly on the frontier, and all the questions were wide open," recalled Alan. He realized that pretty much anything he found out would be an important discovery. Alan Stern was hooked.

Pluto has given up a few of its secrets in the decades since. Its classification was also switched from that of the ninth planet to a dwarf planet. Scientists learned that Pluto has at least five moons as well as a changing atmosphere. But some basic Pluto facts remained a mystery—such as what it looked like, said Alan. "Everything we knew about Pluto came from studying it from billions of miles away." The best telescope pictures of Pluto were blob-like smears of beige and brown. It would take a spacecraft to get a close-up look.

Sending a space probe can change everything. No one knew Mars was a desert planet with huge canyons before the Mariner missions of the 1960s. Io was just one of Jupiter's moons until *Voyager 1* snapped pictures of its pizza-like splotchy surface full of erupting volcanoes in 1979. Space missions rewrite textbooks, and the New Horizons mission will unveil many of Pluto's facts for the first time. "It's like we've plucked a mission out of the nineteen sixties and seventies, a bold first-time exploration," said Alan. "But we're doing it with twenty-first-century technology."

PLUTO AS NEVER
BEFORE SEEN,
THANKS TO
NEW HORIZONS.

FIRST, FASTEST, FARTHEST

Twenty-first-century technology made *New Horizons* the fastest spacecraft ever launched. Advanced modern know-how safely shuttled it to the farthest destination on the longest journey to its primary target of any space mission ever. New Horizons is the first mission to an icy dwarf planet, as well as the first explorer of an entire unknown region of the solar system. The Kuiper belt is an outer zone of strange, small worlds and odd, icy objects beyond Neptune. Pluto is its gatekeeper, and in July 2015, *New Horizons* became the first visitor to this new class of planets. The Kuiper belt is an enormous part of our solar system, but because it's so far away, telescopes weren't powerful enough to see objects there until the 1990s. "It's where this whole new class of planets, called dwarf planets, primarily lie," explained Alan. Exploring the Kuiper belt is like opening a

door to a secret third floor of your home, and you have no idea what's up there. (Read more about the Kuiper belt on page 66.)

New Horizons' cameras have revealed Pluto's surface, which includes deep craters, tall mountains, and vast plains. Ice on Pluto isn't just made of water. There is also nitrogen ice, carbon monoxide frost, and methane snow. Instruments onboard the spacecraft measured the different types of ices that form Pluto's landscape and the gases in its air. Some scientists suspect there might even be an underground ocean there. It will take many years to sort and understand all the information collected. "We don't know what we're going to find," said Alan, smiling. "And that's the best part."

FIRST, A PHONE CALL HOME

Back at the celebration, all eyes were once again glued to television and projection screens. "Ladies and gentlemen," an announcer said. "Pluto as never seen before!" And there it was, in living color! Pluto appeared light orange and tan, with bright areas and dark regions. Some parts looked covered in mountains, and others seemed flat and icy. The clear, detailed photograph looked so real. It was breathtaking. The clapping went on for a long time, and by the time it died down, the photo was all over Twitter, Instagram, Facebook, and other social media. People around the globe were admiring Pluto.

"To see Pluto revealed just before our eyes . . . it's just fantastic!" said Alice Bowman, New Horizons' Mission Operations manager (MOM). "I have to pinch myself. Look what we accomplished!" Her face beamed with pride, but there was a bit of worry there, too. "It's a mix of feeling nervous and proud at the same time." The nervousness was because no one had

"IT'S TRULY AMAZING THAT HUMANKIND CAN GO OUT AND EXPLORE THESE WORLDS," SAID ALICE AFTER THE FLYBY ON JULY 14, 2015.

NEW HORIZONS

NASA's First Mission to the Pluto System

MISSION BRIEF
The Journey to Pluto

FIRST FOR THE HISTORY BOOKS

New Horizons is the first mission

- **to Pluto**
- **to an ice dwarf**
- **to a binary planet**
- **to the Kuiper belt**
- **to an unexplored planet in the 21st century**
- **to carry a student-built instrument to a planet**

**JUPITER –
February 28, 2007:**
Spacecraft grabs a gravity assist boost.

**EARTH –
January 19, 2006:**
New Horizons launches
from Florida.

A MARATHON MISSION

2007–14: *New Horizons* cruises at 30,000 miles (48,280 kilometers) per hour, mostly in hibernation mode.

PLUTO FLYBY – July 14, 2015: Pluto system flyby!

KUIPER BELT – 2019: *New Horizons* is set to visit Kuiper belt object 2014 MU69.

TIMELINE OF PLUTO

4.5 billion years ago   Pluto forms

1930   Clyde Tombaugh discovers the ninth planet at Lowell Observatory in Flagstaff, Arizona, on February 18
Named "Pluto" on May 1, as suggested by eleven-year-old English girl Venetia Burney

1950s   Gerard Kuiper describes the possibility of the Kuiper belt

1978   James W. Christy discovers Pluto's moon Charon, June 22

1989   Pluto Underground pushes for mission to Pluto

1992   David Jewitt and Jane Luu discover the first Kuiper belt object

1996   The Hubble Space Telescope photographs the first surface photos of Pluto

1999   Pluto again becomes the farthest planet from the sun. It had been closer than Neptune since January 21, 1979

2001   Alan Stern gets go-ahead from NASA for New Horizons mission

2005   Icy dwarf planet Eris discovered by Mike Brown's team, January 5

2005   The Hubble Space Telescope images reveal two small moons orbiting Pluto, Hydra and Nix, discovered on June 15 and August 15, respectively

2006   *New Horizons* launches toward Pluto system on January 19

2006   The International Astonomical Union (IAU) reclassifies Pluto on August 24 to dwarf planet

2011   A team led by Mark Showalter discovers a fourth small moon, Kerberos, June 28

2012   A team led by Mark Showalter discovers a fifth small moon, Styx, July 7

2015   *New Horizons* flies by Pluto, July 14

2019   *New Horizons* to visit Kuiper belt object 2014 MU69

heard from the spacecraft since it had sent back the photo the night before. This was as planned, however. *New Horizons'* instruments and antenna are on the same side of the spacecraft. If it was scanning Pluto, its antenna wasn't facing Earth. There couldn't have been any communication until it turned around.

"Right now is closest approach," said Alice. "This is when we get the best science, so we don't want it to point to Earth and talk to us." The spacecraft was working hard to collect all it could while it was nearest to Pluto. It was going through its list of commands, doing what it was programmed to do. Even so, Alice and the rest of the New Horizons team would feel better once the spacecraft checked back in. It was scheduled to send a quick "I'm OK" message a little after four in the afternoon EST. Because Pluto is so far away, that radio signal wouldn't get to Earth until nearly 9:00 in the evening.

Most of the collected information was still on the probe, three billion miles away. If a space rock smashed into it as it flew through Pluto's system of five moons, all of it would be lost. "There's a little bit of drama," admitted Alan, "because this is true exploration. We are flying into the unknown. So stay tuned."

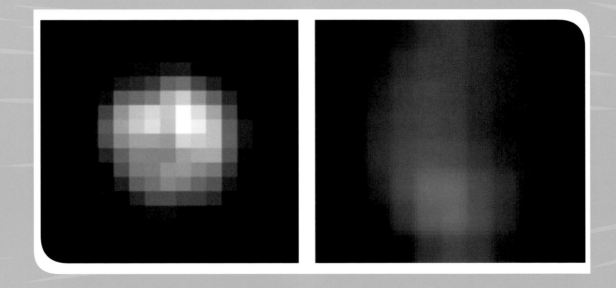

ON THE LEFT IS A PICTURE OF PLUTO TAKEN BY THE HUBBLE SPACE TELESCOPE. (THE COMPUTER-PROCESSED VERSIONS OF THE PICTURE ARE ON PAGE 5.) UNTIL NEW HORIZONS, IT WAS THE BEST VIEW WE HAD OF PLUTO! THE BLOB ON THE RIGHT IS A FAMILIAR OBJECT AT THE SAME RESOLUTION FOR COMPARISON. CAN YOU GUESS WHAT IT IS? (IT'S EARTH!)

TWO

PLUTONIAN DREAMS

Three years after graduating from high school, Clyde Tombaugh was still waiting for his life to begin. Growing up on farms, he'd seen how the backbreaking work didn't guarantee an income, and he'd had his fill of farming. Hadn't a hailstorm just ruined his family's oat and wheat crops, leaving them broke? There would again be no money for Clyde to start college. As the oldest of six kids, he needed to help put food on the table. It looked to Clyde that 1928 would be another lost year.

Clyde turned to his telescope, wondering if his hobby might help him earn some money. He'd built it himself from farm equipment and old car parts. Clyde had even learned to grind the mirrors and lenses on his own, using the thick glass of a ship's porthole window. He had caught the stargazing bug as a young boy from an uncle. Hoping to get some tips on improving his telescope building, he sketched what he saw of Jupiter, Saturn, and Mars through his telescope. Then he wrote up the

CLYDE TOMBAUGH WAS THE FIRST AMERICAN TO DISCOVER A PLANET. AFTER FINDING PLUTO, HE RECEIVED A COLLEGE SCHOLARSHIP AND STUDIED ASTRONOMY.

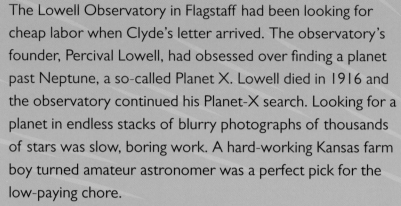

PLANET X

The Lowell Observatory in Flagstaff had been looking for cheap labor when Clyde's letter arrived. The observatory's founder, Percival Lowell, had obsessed over finding a planet past Neptune, a so-called Planet X. Lowell died in 1916 and the observatory continued his Planet-X search. Looking for a planet in endless stacks of blurry photographs of thousands of stars was slow, boring work. A hard-working Kansas farm boy turned amateur astronomer was a perfect pick for the low-paying chore.

Astronomers hunting for planets search the starry night skies for points of light that move. The word *planet* comes from the Greek word for "wanderer." Ancient people knew that these lights in the sky were different from stars. For one, the planets are much closer to us than stars. Planets also circle around the sun, continually changing their positions relative to Earth. Their movements make the planets appear to wander in our night sky against the fixed background of stars.

Night after night Clyde Tombaugh photographed sections of the sky using the Lowell Observatory's new telescope. Then he carefully compared identical sections of the sky, looking for a single point of light that had changed location from one photo to another. That shifting white speck would be Planet X.

On February 18, 1930, Clyde was comparing photographs of a star patch in the constellation Gemini, taken days apart. The twenty-four-year-old noticed a dot of light shift a bit to the left from one photograph to another. Clyde went and found his boss. "I have found your Planet X," he said. Indeed, the young amateur astronomer had discovered Pluto.

observations and mailed them all to an observatory in Arizona.

Clyde's work impressed the observatory's director, so much so that he offered the young man a three-month job. Clyde jumped at the chance and soon boarded a train for the twenty-eight-hour trip to Flagstaff. The journey was exciting, but also a bit overwhelming for a farm kid. Clyde wrote that he found himself a thousand miles from "the treeless plains of Western Kansas," surrounded by strangers, and without "enough money in my wallet for a return ticket home."

AN ODDBALL PLANET

Percival Lowell didn't start looking for a Planet X just out of the blue. He expected to find it because an undiscovered Planet X would explain some wobble that occurred in Neptune's orbit. Neptune itself was discovered because *its* gravity tugs at Uranus. Neptune messes with its neighbor's orbit because it's as big as Uranus. The logic goes that if Planet X is what's pulling at Neptune, then Pluto is about the same size, too. The thinking in the 1930s was that Pluto was a Neptune-like planet.

It turned out that Neptune's orbit doesn't actually have a neighbor-caused wobble. Errors in measurement and math had been made along the way, including overestimating Neptune's mass. There never was a Planet X to be found. Discovering Pluto was sort of an accident, like finding a diamond in the couch while looking for a ring that was never really lost. Pluto probably wouldn't have been found for a few more decades without the Planet X search.

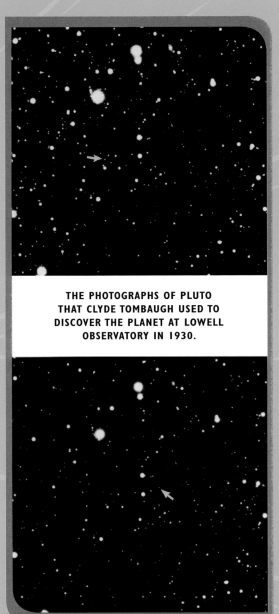

THE PHOTOGRAPHS OF PLUTO THAT CLYDE TOMBAUGH USED TO DISCOVER THE PLANET AT LOWELL OBSERVATORY IN 1930.

THE BLINK COMPARATOR USED BY CLYDE TOMBAUGH. IT'S AN INSTRUMENT THAT SHIFTS AN OBSERVER'S VIEW BACK AND FORTH BETWEEN TWO PHOTOGRAPHS OF THE SAME STAR FIELDS TO DETECT MOVING POINTS OF LIGHT.

Pluto

THE ELEVEN-YEAR-OLD GIRL WHO NAMED PLUTO, VENETIA BURNEY.

Clyde Tombaugh's discovery of a ninth planet was front-page news around the world in 1930. An eleven-year-old girl in England listened closely when her grandfather read the newspaper story to her. Venetia Burney (1918–2009) suggested naming the new planet Pluto, after the Roman god of the underworld. Her grandfather passed along the idea to an astronomer friend, who contacted the Lowell Observatory. Clyde approved of the name, since it started with the initials of Percival Lowell.

IN 2006 AFTER *NEW HORIZONS* WAS LAUNCHED, ALAN STERN VISITED VENETIA BURNEY IN ENGLAND. HE PRESENTED HER WITH A PLAQUE SAYING THAT AN INSTRUMENT ONBOARD WAS NAMED IN HER HONOR, THE VENETIA BURNEY STUDENT DUST COUNTER.

Eventually astronomers realized that Pluto wasn't like Neptune, or any of the other gas giant planets such as Uranus, Jupiter, or Saturn. Nor was Pluto a rocky terrestrial planet like Earth, Venus, Mercury, or Mars. Pluto didn't really fit into either group. "It looked like the solar system consisted of four terrestrial planets, four giant gas planets, and misfit Pluto," said Alan Stern. Pluto's oddball image grew after astronomer James Christy discovered its largest moon in 1978.

Charon is not your average moon. It's huge compared with its planet, about half of Pluto's size. Charon is also close to Pluto, only 12,200 miles (19,600 kilometers) away. Charon makes a lap around Pluto in less than a week. By comparison, the Earth's moon takes four times as long to make an orbit and is twenty times farther away. Even odder is that unlike most moons out there, Charon doesn't exactly orbit Pluto. A moon orbits its planet's center of gravity. Pluto and Charon are so close in size and mass that they both, together, as a single unit orbit a point in space between the pair. They are a double, or binary, planet system. Being close in size and distance also causes Pluto's and Charon's orbits to be double locked, each always showing the same side to the other. They circle around the sun like two spinning dancers who never break eye contact.

The discovery of Charon made Pluto even

PLUTO AND CHARON ARE A BINARY PLANET,
OR DOUBLE PLANET, SYSTEM.

more interesting, and added to the growing list of questions
about the newest planet. Not to worry, thought space scientists, a space probe will surely get a good look at Pluto soon.
After all, it was the 1970s, the golden days of NASA's solar
system exploration. Humans were driving rovers around on
the moon! The terrestrial planets had all been mapped and
photographed. The Pioneer robotic space probes had safely
cut across the asteroid belt and visited Jupiter and Saturn.
Their successors, the *Voyagers,* were set to go farther, in a
grand tour of the solar system. Surely one of them would
make it to Pluto. But it didn't happen that way. *Voyager 1*'s
mission planners decided to skip Pluto in favor of more time
at Saturn. *Voyager 2* would be the first (and so far the last) to
go to Uranus and Neptune, putting it in the wrong direction
to reach Pluto. The littlest planet remained unvisited. Pluto
was left out of the grand tour.

CHARON IS BIG COMPARED WITH PLUTO, BUT BOTH ARE SMALL
WORLDS COMPARED WITH EARTH.

THE PLUTO UNDERGROUND IN 1993. ALAN STERN IS IN THE FRONT, TOWARD THE LEFT, WEARING DARK GLASSES; FRAN BAGENAL IS ON THE FRONT RIGHT, HOLDING A NEWSPAPER.

ABOUT ONE-FOURTH OF THE NEW HORIZONS TEAM IS FEMALE. FRAN BAGENAL IS STANDING ON THE FAR LEFT, AND ALICE BOWMAN ON THE FAR RIGHT.

Italian restaurants aren't unusual in Baltimore. But the dinnertime conversation inside one on a May evening in 1989 was anything but usual. Alan Stern had gathered together a group of planetary scientists and astronomers that night. All were in town for science meetings and had heard a lecture on Pluto. Many grumbled about the Voyager missions passing up Pluto. Imagine how much more we'd know about Pluto and Charon if a spacecraft had visited them!

Pluto is just too far away to study in detail from Earth. "We wanted a mission that would get out there and make observations of this object on the edge of the solar system," explained Fran Bagenal, a planetary scientist. "We needed to get NASA behind a mission to Pluto," Alan agreed. By the time the dozen scientists had paid their bill that night, they were calling themselves the Pluto Underground. A movement was born. "I was a part of it because how could you *not* be?" said Alan. "How could you *not* want to be a part of the exploration of a whole new world?"

"We started a campaign to get a mission to Pluto," recalled Fran Bagenal about that night. She admitted that at first she thought Alan might be a bit crazy. Send a spacecraft to just faraway Pluto? That was going to be a hard sell. But Fran and the other young scientists knew that the Kuiper belt was the next great frontier of exploration. "Pluto is a very exciting place," said Fran. "This little thing at the edge of the solar system" represents all that Kuiper belt stuff left over from the formation of the solar system.

Getting NASA to back a Pluto mission took many years. If they'd known then how much time, work, and disappointment were ahead of them, Alan said, "we probably would not

WHAT'S IN A NAME?

Charon

Pluto's partner moon is Charon. The American astronomer James Christy discovered it in 1978 and proposed its name. Charon was the mythological boatman who ferried souls across the river Styx, which surrounds Pluto's underworld. Some pronounce the moon's name like *Sharon* or *Karen*. But Christy chose the name because it's similar to *Charlene*, his wife's name, and so he pronounces it *shahr-on*.

PLUTO'S LARGEST MOON, CHARON.

MISSION BRIEF

Pluto Primer

SMALLISH PLANET, BIG DWARF

- Pluto is about 1,473 miles (2,370 kilometers) across, a bit smaller than Earth's moon.

- Pluto's mass is 1.3×10^{22} kilograms, about .0022 of the Earth's.

- On Pluto you would weigh about one-fifteenth of what you do on Earth. A 75-pound kid would weigh 6 pounds.

- Pluto is one of the largest and brightest Kuiper belt objects and a big icy dwarf planet.

LOONY MOON

- Charon is about 745 miles (1,200 kilometers) in diameter, about the size of Texas.

- It's made of ice and rock and covered in a surface of mostly water ice, but it has no known atmosphere.

- Charon orbits Pluto once every 6.4 days. That's the same amount of time as its day, or how long it takes to rotate once.

- Charon is only 12,200 miles (19,600 kilometers) away from Pluto.

- Pluto also has four tiny moons named Nix, Hydra, Styx, and Kerberos. (Read more about them in the Mission Brief on page 44.)

DOUBLE PLANET

- Charon and Pluto are the moon-planet pair most similar in size to each other in the entire solar system.

- They are a binary planet system, orbiting around a point in space between the pair called a barycenter.

- Pluto's and Charon's orbits are double locked, too, each body always showing the same side to the other.

- If you were standing on Pluto and looking up, Charon would be easy to find. It always hovers in the same place in the sky. Ditto for standing on Charon and looking at Pluto.

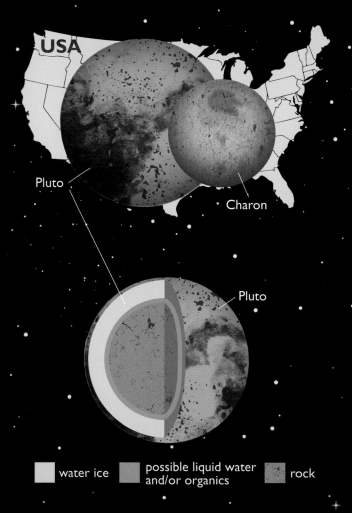

USA

Pluto

Charon

Pluto

water ice
possible liquid water and/or organics
rock

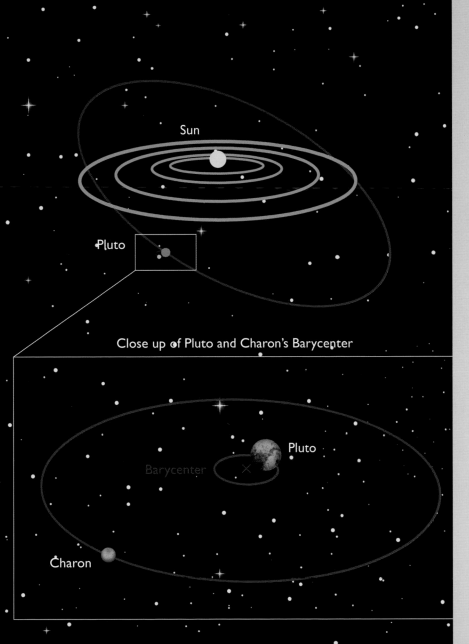

Sun

Pluto

Close up of Pluto and Charon's Barycenter

Barycenter ✕

Pluto

Charon

COLD, ICY, AND FAR AWAY

- Pluto is, on average, 3.7 billion miles (5.9 billion kilometers) from the sun, nearly forty times farther away than Earth.

- One trip around the sun, a Pluto year, lasts 248 Earth years. Say goodbye to birthdays!

- A day on Pluto goes on for 153 hours and 18 minutes. Pluto spins backwards and nearly over on its side, like a bead on a string.

- Pluto's 248-year journey around the sun isn't a perfect circle. Its egg-shaped orbit takes it billions of miles farther from the sun than at other times during a Pluto year.

- Pluto's orbit is not on the same plane as the eight major planets; it's tilted at an angle to it.

- For about 20 years within each 248-year orbit, Pluto is actually closer to the sun than Neptune is. This was true between 1979 and 1999.

- Temperatures are between -396 and -360 degrees Fahrenheit (-238 and -218 degrees Celsius).

- Pluto is about two-thirds rock and one-third ice. It has a rocky center surrounded by a shell of hard-as-bedrock water ice and a top layer of nitrogen, carbon monoxide, and methane ices.

- Its atmosphere is mostly nitrogen (like Earth's), with traces of methane and carbon monoxide.

- Seasons are extreme on Pluto because of its severe tilt and odd orbit. In the winter, Pluto gets less than half of the sunlight that it gets in the summer.

- Pluto's ices evaporate more when it's closer to the sun, and add to the atmosphere. Once it moves away from the sun and cools, those gases condense into snow that falls and becomes ice again.

- Pluto's atmospheric surface pressure is currently about 100,000 times less than on Earth, about 600 times less than on Mars.

UNIVERSITY OF COLORADO
PROFESSOR AND PLANETARY
ASTRONOMER FRAN BAGENAL.

television shows featured the story, and the public got involved. A Pennsylvania high school student started a Save the Pluto Mission campaign that sent thousands of protest letters NASA's way.

The space agency decided to try again. It opened a new competition, asking for mission ideas and plans that would study Pluto and the Kuiper belt before 2020. "We are the undead," Alan responded.

NASA had other rules besides getting there by 2020. To qualify, a Pluto mission had to be cheap, costing no more than $500 million. That's a slim budget for a project that would probably take fifteen years to complete and require a spacecraft to fly three billion miles. NASA didn't want risky, untested, or untried technology either. No far-fetched proton engines or wacky balloon landers. "Everything had to be the safest, the surest bet," Alan said. He and others in the Pluto Underground joined up with scientists at the Applied Physics Laboratory (APL) at the Johns Hopkins University in Maryland. Together they made a plan for a mission with a small, simple ship packed with cameras and science instruments. It would get to Pluto in nine years thanks to a big rocket and a boost from Jupiter.

NASA announced its selection in late 2001. New Horizons had won! A NASA mission to Pluto was finally a go. There wasn't much time to celebrate. The team had only forty-two months to turn a sketch of a spacecraft into *New Horizons*. If they couldn't get it built, tested, and launched before February 2006, it wouldn't arrive at Jupiter in time for its needed boost. There was a small window of time for everything to happen right. And that window was closing fast. The race to the launch pad was on.

have had the courage to take on the task." But an astonishing number of people hung in there, including Fran. She and many others from that initial meeting are, twenty-five years later, on the New Horizons team.

The list of Pluto missions that never got off the drawing board during the 1990s is long. It includes Pluto 350, Pluto Fast Flyby, and Pluto Express. Then there was Pluto-Kuiper Express, a mission that was expected to be launched around 2004. It was almost built, but in 2000, as its budget swelled to a billion dollars, NASA declared the mission to be "over, canceled, dead."

That cancellation got a lot of pushback, and not just from scientists. Members of Congress complained that the taxpayers had gotten nothing for all the money that had already been spent on the abandoned mission. Newspapers, magazines, and

Three

BUILT TO GO
THE DISTANCE

Outer space may be quiet, but NASA's Space Environment Simulator (SES) in Greenbelt, Maryland, is not. The three-story-high metal chamber is covered in gurgling pipes, hissing valves, and churning pumps. In 2005 a robotic probe scheduled to depart for Pluto in five months was inside the SES. Engineers were testing *New Horizons'* space worthiness. Inside the SES chamber is a little bit of outer space, or at least space-like conditions.

Chris Hersman waited nearby as temperatures inside the airless chamber were chilled down to nearly –300 degrees Fahrenheit (–184 degrees Celsius). Chris is the lead engineer for the New Horizons mission and a longtime space guy. "I remember being in a space club in third grade and we had to pick who got to be the astronaut," Chris recalled. "I always had an interest in computers and space," said the electrical engineer. He made sure that *New Horizons* was built to be tough. Surviving the strain of a launch and the harsh environment of space takes

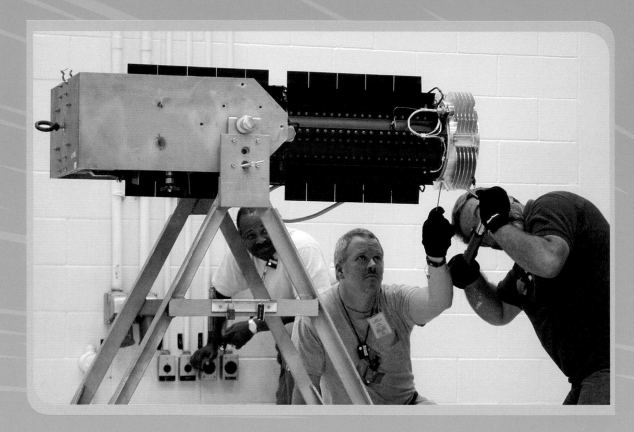

extreme engineering. By then, NASA staff had bombarded the spacecraft with rocket-level noise in a sound chamber, shook it at blastoff strength on vibration tables, and spun it around on a big wheel. Now the spacecraft was spending forty days sealed in an airless vacuum inside the SES. And being frozen.

The purpose of the tests was to flush out problems. There are no space-walking astronaut repair crews where *New Horizons* is going. Better to push equipment to the breaking point on Earth while a fix could still be figured out. The low temperatures inside the SES proved to be too much for one piece of electronics. One of the circuit boards got "fritzy" in the cold, and it had to be replaced with a different kind. "There's more than one solution when you build a spacecraft," said

Chris. "It's kind of like a puzzle you put together." A high-stakes puzzle with a high-pressure deadline. Swapping out and retesting electronics burns up both time and money. A delay in the scheduled launch would add years to *New Horizons'* journey.

DARK, COLD, AND FAR

The *New Horizons* spacecraft was a design challenge. "We had to build a spacecraft to fly so far from Earth, to operate so far from home, as well as so far from the sun—and one that can take care of itself," said Alan Stern. First on the list of spacecraft must-haves was power. Solar panels make electricity for most satellites and space probes. But a sunny day on Pluto is about as bright as twilight on Earth. With only one-thousandth of the sun's energy

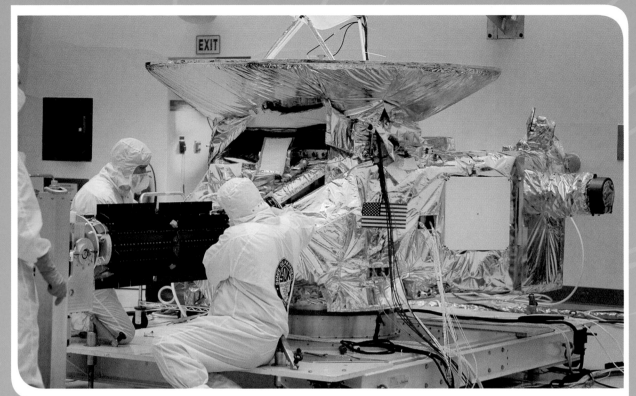

reaching that far, *New Horizons* couldn't go solar. The spacecraft had to carry its own power source.

"What we have onboard is a radioisotope thermoelectric generator [RTG]," explained Chris. "Inside the RTG is about 24 pounds [11 kilograms] of plutonium." That's right, *plutonium* powers the first Pluto probe! Plutonium is a radioactive element. As it breaks down over time, or decays, it gives off heat. The RTG uses that heat to make electricity, which runs the spacecraft's computers and instruments.

New Horizons is a marvel of energy efficiency. The entire spacecraft uses less electricity than a few regular light bulbs. Heat from the plutonium warms things up, too. "It's almost room temperature inside the spacecraft," said Chris. *New*

Horizons' compact shape and its gold-colored insulating blanket hold in the warmth, keeping heat from escaping into space. Even the heat given off by its working electronics is trapped inside, like hot soup in a thermos.

The RTG powers only the electronics, not the spacecraft itself. Hard as it is to believe, no engine sends the spacecraft traveling 33,000 miles (53,000 kilometers) per hour through space. All of its forward motion comes from the rocket that launched it from Earth and a later boost from Jupiter's gravity. *New Horizons'* ability to steer comes from a tank of liquid propellant. It fuels small jet thrusters that turn and maneuver the spacecraft.

TOUGH AND LIGHTWEIGHT

Squeezing the maximum speed from the rocket launch required cutting back on the craft's weight. "To get to Pluto quickly we had to be very light," said Chris. *New Horizons* weighs a slim 1,054 pounds (478 kilograms), about the weight and size of a large grand piano. Its metal frame is made of honeycomb-like aluminum cells covered in foil sheets, not solid metal panels. These sheets are just as strong as metal panels and nearly 90 percent lighter. The science instruments were specially made, too. "All seven together weigh less than one camera aboard the *Cassini* orbiter at Saturn," said Alan. *New Horizons* is lightweight, yet tough enough to survive the shake of a blasting rocket and a decade in space.

ASLEEP AND ALONE

New Horizons has spent years flying with many of its systems powered down. It's called hibernation mode. "When we reach Pluto after nine and a half years of flight . . . many of the electronics will be less than three years old because it's been sleeping most of the time," explained Alan. Hibernation mode saves wear and tear on the spacecraft, as well as time and money. Team members worked on other projects instead of babysit-

CHRIS HERSMAN, LEAD ENGINEER FOR NEW HORIZONS, USES A MODEL OF THE SPACECRAFT TO EXPLAIN HOW IT WORKS.

ting *New Horizons* during its decade en route. "Hibernation is probably the safest mode of operation for the spacecraft," said Chris. It doesn't fly in multiple directions; instead it continually turns in a nice, stable spin. Its antenna points toward Earth in case it needs to communicate. Because the spacecraft isn't really controlling anything, "very little can go wrong," said Chris.

The spacecraft was built to take care of itself. One way of doing that was loading it up with extra parts. "There's two of nearly everything," said Alan: two computers, two data recorders, extra thrusters, backup electronics, and extra fuel. The spacecraft builders also avoided using moving parts. Any piece of machinery that moves will eventually break. *New Horizons* doesn't have any moving arms or rotating instruments.

Another reason the spacecraft needs to be self-sufficient is the long lag time in communications. A call for help doesn't accomplish much when Earth is so far away. Radio signals travel at the speed of light. That sounds fast, but it takes nine hours for a Pluto-originated message to be received and answered in the United States. A lot can happen in nine hours. Any spacecraft alert that shows up at the Mission Operations Center is already old news. "It happened four and a half hours ago, and it will take us another four and a half hours to do anything about it," explained Chris.

"The spacecraft is really on its own," agreed Alan. "If something goes wrong, it is the software that has to take over and care for the spacecraft." Chris and the engineering team programmed *New Horizons'* computers with an autonomy system. "It's a list of rules," explained Chris, rules that automatically execute specific commands for particular problem

Fast Spacecraft, Slow Downlink

Making a fast, skinny spacecraft required skimping on some things, including data download speed. It takes a while for *New Horizons* to send its measurements and pictures back to Earth. Why? It has a small antenna and limited electrical power.

The dish antenna is about 7 feet (2.1 meters) across. "If you stretch your arms out in both directions, it's about that big," said Chris. That's not gigantic, considering it has to send and receive radio signals from 3 billion miles (5 billion kilometers) away. The antennas on the *Voyagers* are nearly twice that long. Because *New Horizons* is equipped with a single small RTG, it has low-power transmitters, too.

The collected and stored information and images trickle back to Earth. Just how slow is the downlink? On average one kilobit per second, or a thousand times slower than a smartphone. "You couldn't stand to read your email at that speed," said Alan. "It'll take an hour to send back one compressed picture." It was almost 2017 by the time *New Horizons* finished sending back all the data it collected during its 2015 flyby of the Pluto system.

MISSION BRIEF
The Spacecraft

The *New Horizons* spacecraft is about 8 feet (2.5 meters) across and weighs 1,050 pounds (480 kilograms). It's about the size of a large grand piano. It carries seven scientific instruments: Alice, Ralph, SDC, SWAP, PEPSSI, REX, and LORRI.

LORRI, the **L**ong-**R**ange **R**econnaissance **I**mager, snaps the sharpest, closest, and highest-resolution photos yet of Pluto. This eagle-eyed telescopic camera's images can reveal features that are as small as a football field.

SWAP is the **S**olar **W**ind **A**round **P**luto, an instrument that measures the solar wind at Pluto, searching for a magnetosphere, and studying how quickly Pluto's atmosphere is escaping into space.

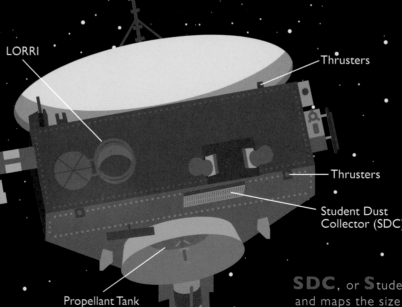

LORRI

Thrusters

SWAP

Thrusters

Student Dust Collector (SDC)

Propellant Tank

SDC, or **S**tudent **D**ust **C**ounter, measures and maps the size and number of impacts with dust particles as *New Horizons* crosses the solar system. By studying the distribution of dust left over from the formation of the solar system, the student-built instrument will teach us more about how planets form.

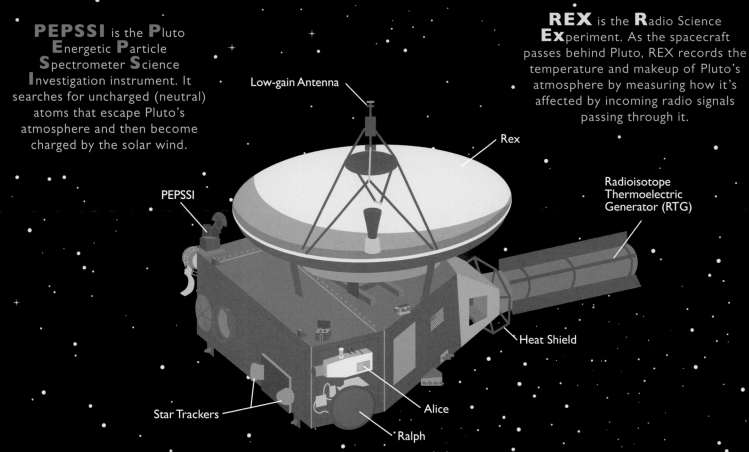

PEPSSI is the **P**luto **E**nergetic **P**article **S**pectrometer **S**cience **I**nvestigation instrument. It searches for uncharged (neutral) atoms that escape Pluto's atmosphere and then become charged by the solar wind.

REX is the **R**adio Science **Ex**periment. As the spacecraft passes behind Pluto, REX records the temperature and makeup of Pluto's atmosphere by measuring how it's affected by incoming radio signals passing through it.

Low-gain Antenna

Rex

PEPSSI

Radioisotope Thermoelectric Generator (RTG)

Heat Shield

Star Trackers

Alice

Ralph

Ralph is a color camera that takes pictures and makes maps that show what Pluto's surface is made of. Its infrared thermal maps show cooler and warmer regions.

Alice studies Pluto's atmosphere, measuring and mapping the kinds and amounts of chemicals and gases and their temperatures at different levels above the planet. It's an ultraviolet imaging spectrometer, an instrument that breaks up light into a rainbow, like a prism, to create an image in the ultraviolet.

27

New Horizons

Alan Stern chose the name New Horizons for the mission and spacecraft. Why? "We were seeking new horizons to explore at Pluto and Charon and the Kuiper belt," he wrote. A few of the rejected names were Tombaugh Explorer, X, New Worlds Explorer, and One Giant Leap.

situations without asking a human for advice or permission. The onboard autonomy system constantly monitors data on the spacecraft, alerting itself to anything out of the ordinary and fixing it. "It's pretty impressive stuff," said Alan. "I am always in awe of what the engineers have done."

LOOKING FOR ICE AND AIR, PARTICLES AND DUST

As impressive as the *New Horizons* spacecraft is, it alone can't tell us anything about Pluto. That's the job of the seven science instruments onboard. They are like the sense organs of the

mission, seeing, hearing, tasting, smelling, and touching the Pluto system for us. "It's the most powerful payload ever sent on a first reconnaissance to a planet in the history of space exploration," said Alan. Powerful in the amount of science it can do.

Let's start with the eyes. "We have a camera called LORRI that takes high-resolution pictures," said planetary scientist Fran Bagenal. LORRI takes sharp black-and-white pictures of Pluto's surface from far off while "Ralph [another camera] takes wide-angle pictures in color." The Ralph camera sees in four different color wavelengths. Seeing in different colors will reveal what Pluto's surface is made of, said Fran. "We'll figure out what that brown stuff is. Is it rock? Or is it organic material?"

Ralph also takes images in invisible infrared, sensing heat like night-vision goggles. "The infrared part of the spectrum is particularly good for working out different kinds of ices," said Fran. There's more than one kind of ice on Pluto. "There is carbon dioxide ice, methane ice, nitrogen ice," explained the planetary scientist. Each element has a unique fingerprint that the instrument can identify by breaking up its light into colors.

The third "seeing" instrument captures light invisible to us on the opposite end of the spectrum, which we can't see. "Alice is an ultraviolet instrument," said Fran. When *New Horizons* flew behind Pluto and looked back at the sun, Alice imaged the sunlight coming through its atmosphere. "That will tell us the composition of the atmosphere, the pressure of the atmosphere, the . . . temperature of the atmosphere, all those things." Not just what gases are in Pluto's air, but how much nitrogen, methane, and carbon dioxide there is at each level.

Another instrument for probing Pluto's atmosphere is REX, or Radio Science Experiment. It's part of *New Horizons'*

NEW HORIZONS GETS ITS EAGLE-EYED TELESCOPIC CAMERA, LORRI.

THE LORRI CAMERA TAKES
CLOSE-UPS, BUT ONLY IN
BLACK-AND-WHITE.

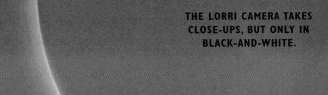

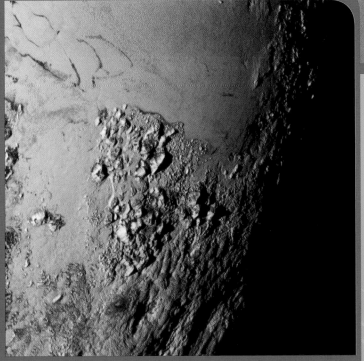

NEW HORIZONS' SWAP
INSTRUMENT STUDIED
SOLAR WIND INTERACTIONS
AT PLUTO.

WHAT'S IN A NAME?

Ralph and Alice

Science instruments need names that are easy to use and not confusing. Five of the science instruments on *New Horizons* are abbreviations or acronyms, names made out of the first letters of their full names. SWAP stands for Solar Wind Around Pluto, for example. To keep things simple, Ralph and Alice were named after the main characters in the 1950s television show *The Honeymooners*.

NEW HORIZONS' SCIENCE GOALS: THE BIG THREE

- **Get a close-up look.** What does the terrain of Pluto and Charon look like close-up?

- **Map the surface.** What kinds of ices and rock make up the surfaces of Pluto and Charon?

- **Study Pluto's atmosphere.** What gases is Pluto's atmosphere made of, and how long will it last?

big dish antenna. "We use the radio antenna to communicate with Earth," explained Fran. It delivers all the pictures and information to Earth. "But we'll also use that antenna to measure the radio signals that go through the atmosphere of Pluto.

"We also have two particle instruments. One is SWAP [Solar Wind Around Pluto], and another instrument called PEPSSI [Pluto Energetic Particle Spectrometer Science Investigation]," said Fran. SWAP measures how the solar wind from the faraway sun interacts with Pluto. PEPSSI measures similar particles that escape from Pluto's atmosphere and are then carried away by the solar wind. "We'll get a sense of the total amount of material that is being lost from the atmosphere of Pluto."

The seventh instrument counts dust. "Dust is really important," said Fran. Space dust is made of bits of broken-up space objects such as asteroids, comets, and Kuiper belt objects. The Student Dust Counter (SDC) records each dust bit that

strikes it as it moves through space. There is surprisingly little space dust between the planets. Only a few microscopic dust particles hit the SDC every week.

Fran is super proud of the University of Colorado students who built the SDC. She's a professor at the university. Fran said the project gave college students "hands-on experience in designing, building, and operating space hardware that actually flies into space." That's a rare opportunity. What else? "It inspires kids to study science and do their math homework and get excited and enthusiastic about space, particularly Pluto."

Fran, like Alan Stern, was inspired by the moon landings. "As a teenager in rural England," she said, "I stayed up through the middle of the night to watch the Apollo astronauts walk on the moon." Her love of planetary science brought her to the United States. Colorado is also a great place for rock climbing and skiing, two of her other passions. Fran has worked

Seeing Across the Spectrum

Light is vibrating waves of electric and magnetic fields that travel at a speed of 186,000 miles (300,000 kilometers) per second. The part of the electromagnetic spectrum that human eyes can see is the wavelengths of visible light. Scientific instruments, like those onboard *New Horizons*, can detect other wavelengths. Like an x-ray picture, these instruments create images out of invisible light that reveal information. The different views of the Crab Nebula, below, are a good example.

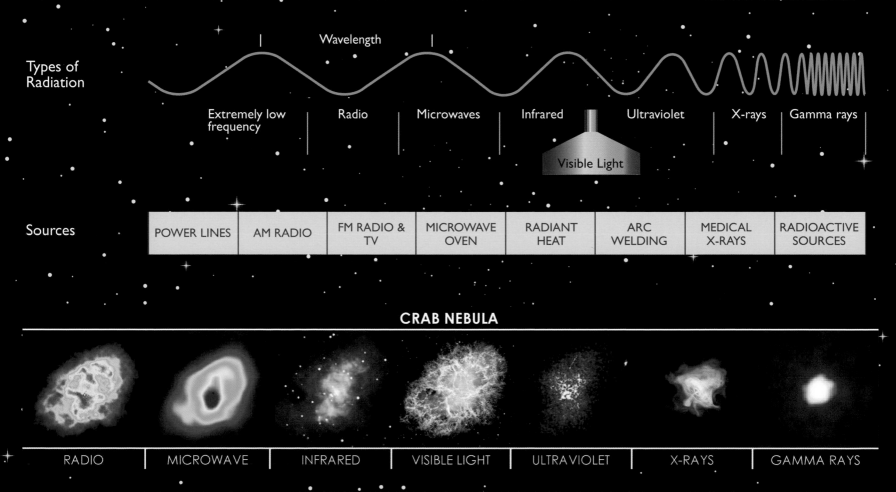

Wavelength

Types of Radiation

Extremely low frequency | Radio | Microwaves | Infrared | Ultraviolet | X-rays | Gamma rays

Visible Light

Sources	POWER LINES	AM RADIO	FM RADIO & TV	MICROWAVE OVEN	RADIANT HEAT	ARC WELDING	MEDICAL X-RAYS	RADIOACTIVE SOURCES

CRAB NEBULA

RADIO	MICROWAVE	INFRARED	VISIBLE LIGHT	ULTRAVIOLET	X-RAYS	GAMMA RAYS

THE CRAB NEBULA IS THE CLOUDY REMAINS OF A ONCE MASSIVE STAR THAT BECAME A SUPERNOVA. NOTICE HOW DIFFERENT IT LOOKS IN VISIBLE LIGHT COMPARED WITH INFRARED (HEAT) AND HOW IMAGES IN THE SHORTER WAVELENGTHS REVEAL THE TINY DENSE NEUTRON STAR THAT IS NOW AT ITS CORE.

FRAN BAGENAL IS STUDYING HOW THE SOLAR WIND INTERACTS WITH PLUTO'S ESCAPING ATMOSPHERE.

ALAN STERN SAYS GOODBYE TO *NEW HORIZONS* FROM THE LAUNCH PAD IN 2006.

on a number of NASA missions, including the Voyagers and the Jupiter orbiter *Juno*. There are lots of ways to work in space science, said Fran. "Mission design, mission operations, data analysis, modeling. . . . It's a great job."

AT LAST, A LAUNCH

Tuesday, January 17, 2006, was supposed to be the big day. The *New Horizons* spacecraft waited patiently from its perch atop a 200-foot (61-meter) Atlas V rocket sitting on the launch pad at Cape Canaveral. A number of New Horizons team members traveled to Florida for the sendoff of the Pluto probe. The daughter and wife of Clyde Tombaugh were also there. The

discoverer of Pluto had died nine years earlier to the day. Some of his ashes were onboard the spacecraft in his honor.

Unfortunately, bad weather killed Tuesday's launch. The speed of wind gusts near the ground was over the safety limit. NASA rescheduled the launch for the next day. The same storm that had brought Tuesday's winds caused a power outage that scrubbed Wednesday's blastoff. "We all know these things happen with launches," said Fran Bagenal. "But when it's your baby, you just want it to go, and go now."

Thursday wasn't looking likely either. Cloudiness had already caused a delay in the morning. But at around noon on January 19, 2006, the sky cleared. The launch was back on!

NEW HORIZONS IS THE FASTEST SPACECRAFT EVER LAUNCHED. IT PASSED THE MOON IN ONLY NINE HOURS! IT TOOK ASTRONAUTS THREE DAYS TO MAKE THAT JOURNEY. *NEW HORIZONS* REACHED JUPITER IN JUST THIRTEEN MONTHS.

NEW HORIZONS GOT OFF TO A FAST START THANKS TO A BIG ROCKET CARRYING THIS SMALL, LIGHTWEIGHT SPACECRAFT.

NEW HORIZONS WAS LAUNCHED ATOP AN ATLAS V ROCKET ON JANUARY 19, 2006.

33

Soon a voice on the loudspeaker began counting down. "Ten, nine, eight. . . ."

Alan Stern dashed out of the sound-protected room onto the observation deck. "I didn't wait seventeen years not to be outside and hear this thunder away from Earth," he said.

"Five, four, three, two, one. We have ignition and liftoff of NASA's *New Horizons* spacecraft on a decade-long voyage to visit the planet Pluto, and then beyond!"

"I will never forget it if I live to be a hundred and fifty," said Alan. "I just looked up at that rocket and I said to myself, 'Make us proud, baby. Go get 'em.'"

After a nerve-racking forty-five minutes, the spacecraft

A HAPPY FRAN BAGENAL IN FLORIDA FOR THE LAUNCH OF *NEW HORIZONS* IN 2006.

SPACECRAFT STOWAWAYS

The New Horizons team included these nine mementos onboard the Pluto-bound probe:

- Two U.S. flags

- State quarters from Florida—the launch site—and from APL's home state of Maryland

- A 1991 U.S. stamp of Pluto with the label "Not Yet Explored"

- A piece of the historic *SpaceShipOne*

- Some of Clyde Tombaugh's ashes

- A CD with pictures of team members

- A CD with more than 434,000 names that people submitted to a "Send Your Name to Pluto" project in 2005 (including this author!)

separated from the rocket and checked in with Earth. "Once you talk to the spacecraft and see that everything onboard is fine, it's a huge relief," said engineer Chris Hersman.

"All I can say is yeeeee-ha!" a smiling Fran told reporters that day. "I have to keep pinching myself to believe it's really happened."

New Horizons was on its own, headed for Pluto. Now the team would have to spend the next nine years making sure it got there.

SPRINTING ACROSS THE SOLAR SYSTEM

The Mission Operations Center for *New Horizons* was busy the night of December 6, 2014. It was seven months before flyby, but the center crawled with people working on laptops and fidgeting with smartphones. The wall clock read nine thirty. Flight controllers scooted around on wheeled chairs between computer terminals. The screens glowed with colorful diagrams and columns of numbers that kept changing, like a stopwatch.

Live data also appeared on two overhead monitors the size of big-screen TVs. A third large screen showed a computerized image of a spacecraft against a background of black space. Everyone was waiting to hear from this small robotic probe. *New Horizons* had spent most of the previous nine years speeding through space at 9 miles (14 kilometers) per *second*. Now it was time for *New Horizons* to wake up and get to work. Its destination was only months away.

NEW HORIZONS FLIGHT CONTROLLERS MONITOR INCOMING TELEMETRY FROM THE DISTANT PLUTO-BOUND SPACECRAFT.

NEW HORIZONS

NASA's First Mission to the Pl...

ALICE BOWMAN IS NEW HORIZONS' MISSION
OPERATIONS MANAGER, OR MOM.

THE MOM (MISSION OPERATIONS MANAGER) ALICE BOWMAN AND THE OPERATIONS TEAM
WAIT TO HEAR BACK FROM *NEW HORIZONS* THE NIGHT OF DECEMBER 6, 2014.

Inside the Mission Operations Center, Alice Bowman wore a headset and sat staring at her computer. Then she turned, smiled, and gave a thumbs-up. The Mission Operations manager, or MOM, flipped on the speaker. "MOM on Pluto 1," Alice said. "We have . . . wake-up of the *New Horizons* spacecraft on our way to Pluto." People clapped and smiled in relief. "It's game time!" said Alan Stern. The exploration of the Kuiper belt was about to begin. "This has been a very long road."

A LONG CRUISE

Alice Bowman knows perfectly well how long the journey has been. "We used to joke when we first started this mission that we could send a command to the spacecraft and then go to the restroom," said Alice. The five minutes it took *New Horizons* to answer was enough for a bathroom break. By 2007 a response from the spacecraft took ninety minutes. Plenty of time for lunch between command and response. With the spacecraft nearly at Pluto, turnaround time had grown to nine hours. "Now we have enough time to go home and sleep," joked Alice. Pluto is a very long way from Earth.

Alice has been *New Horizons'* Mission Operations manager since the start. And she was a space scientist for years before that. As with others on the team, growing up while astronauts explored the moon made a big impression on her. Shows such as *Star Trek* and *Lost in Space* got her imagination going, too. "I was a space-geek kind of kid," she said. There's a lamp in the shape of the *Enterprise* in her office to prove it.

As MOM, Alice works with both Pluto scientists and *New Horizons* engineers and flight controllers. Her job is to understand what exactly scientists want to learn—what's in Pluto's atmosphere, the kinds of ices, and so on—and figure out how the spacecraft can find that out. "I need to know the spacecraft's capabilities, what it can and can't do," explained Alice. She turns the wish list of observations into spacecraft commands. These instruct *New Horizons* to take pictures, analyze the air, or map the surface. Alice must also coordinate spacecraft communication with the Deep Space Network. It's NASA's system of giant satellite-dish antennas around the world that all space missions share. If the Deep Space Network isn't receiving what *New Horizons* is sending, none of it matters much.

NASA'S GIANT DEEP SPACE NETWORK ANTENNA IN GOLDSTONE, CALIFORNIA, CAN COMMUNICATE WITH SPACECRAFT THAT ARE 10 BILLION MILES (16 BILLION KILOMETERS) AWAY.

"Everything needs to play nice together," said Alice.

Flying a spacecraft so far for so long has challenges. "We've had to be very good stewards of the spacecraft," said Alan, and at the same time be planning the encounter with Pluto. Hibernation mode has helped New Horizons' small team get it all done. The spacecraft has slept away many years of the long cruise toward the edge of the solar system. During hibernation mode, New Horizons checked in every Monday. It would send a green beacon if all was OK and a red beacon if a problem needed reporting, like a computer that had rebooted itself. The spacecraft also got checkups. The team woke it up at least once a year to run tests to make sure it was healthy when they needed to upload new commands or fire thrusters to correct its course.

Keeping New Horizons on course was important. Pluto is a tricky target. After traveling 3 billion miles (5 billion kilometers) for nine and a half years, the spacecraft had to hit an exact spot at just the right time. It needed to fly through an area the size of a 60-by-90-mile box (97 by 145 kilometers) within a hundred-second time window. It's equivalent to shooting an arrow and hitting a moving dime a hundred miles away.

What would have happened if the spacecraft missed and

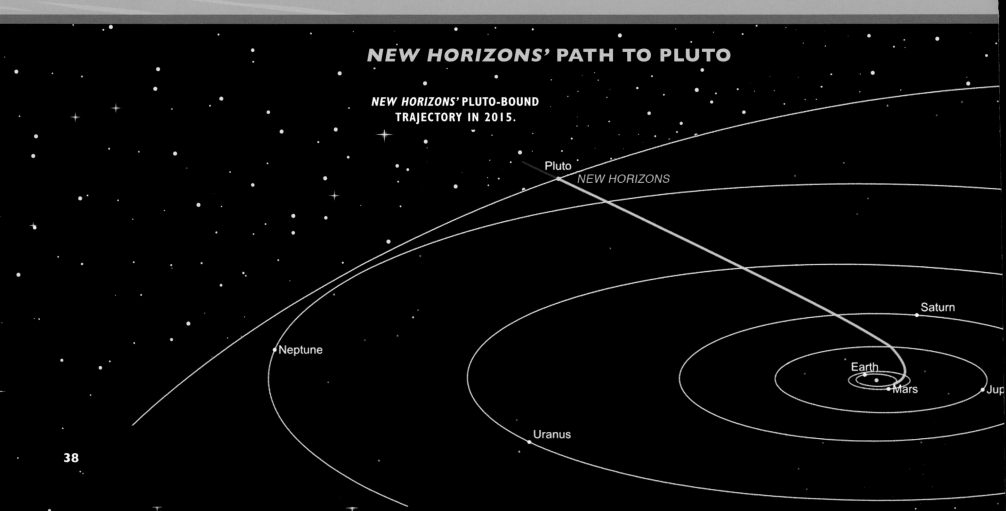

NEW HORIZONS' PATH TO PLUTO

NEW HORIZONS' **PLUTO-BOUND TRAJECTORY IN 2015.**

Pluto

NEW HORIZONS

Saturn

Neptune

Earth

Mars

Jup

Uranus

Pluto Flyby
July 2015

		35-55 km			
	26.8	(18-28 miles)	40%	Oct 2018	43.3 AU
	26.3	35-55 km			
		(22-34 miles)	40%		
	26.4	35-55 km	40%	Apr 2019	44.1 AU
		(22-34 miles)			

ALAN REVIEWS ALTERNATE TRAJECTORIES WITH THE TEAM. "WE WANT PEOPLE TO UNDERSTAND JUST HOW INTERESTING AND HOW NAIL BITING *NEW HORIZONS'* MISSION MIGHT BE," HE SAID. "THIS IS PART OF THE EXCITEMENT OF FIRST-TIME EXPLORATION, OF GOING TO A NEW FRONTIER."

arrived a minute late, or was a bit outside that box? In that case, "the spacecraft's instruments might take many images and spectra of blank sky instead of Pluto or Charon," explained Alan. It's like snapping a picture of a moving motorcycle while riding in a car. Hit the shutter button a second too late and you get nothing. Aim the camera too far to the left and you get a blurry highway. *New Horizons* had to arrive at precisely the right time not just to snap pictures of Pluto, but also to be in alignment with the Deep Space Network's antenna. Nothing really matters if the pictures and science aren't delivered to Earth. It's a complicated performance, so the New Horizons team rehearsed it. "It [was] to get us ready and practiced for the one and only shot we'll have to explore the Pluto system," said Alan.

PRACTICE MAKES PERFECT

During "encounter rehearsal," everything was exactly like the 2015 flyby. The team worked at Mission Operations from seven a.m. to eleven p.m. for nine full days, just like during the Pluto encounter. The spacecraft's onboard computer was made to believe it was at Pluto. *New Horizons* did all its encounter maneuvers—turning on cameras, pointing toward Charon, and sending information back to Earth. The Mission Operations team guided the spacecraft using incoming navigation information to adjust its path when necessary. Science team members pulled the newly downloaded data collected from the observations and studied it just like they would during the Pluto encounter.

A Funny Thing Happened on the Way to Pluto

ERIS

As *New Horizons* was crossing the asteroid belt in August 2006, an auditorium full of people voted on what to call Pluto. The International Astronomical Union (IAU) is the scientific organization in charge of naming planets, moons, and other space objects. The IAU voted to create a new category of space objects called dwarf planets. With a show of hands, the solar system went from having nine planets to having eight, plus three dwarf planets. Pluto was declared a dwarf planet along with the biggest asteroid, Ceres, as well as a newly discovered large Kuiper belt object (KBO) called Eris.

Eris's discovery is what led to the vote. When astronomer Mike Brown found it in 2005, he announced that Eris was the tenth planet. (At the time Pluto was the ninth.) This caused an uproar and set off a fierce debate. Many astronomers considered Eris a big KBO, not a planet. But Pluto is also a big KBO, so if Eris wasn't a planet, how could Pluto be one? On the other hand, if Pluto was the ninth planet and Eris the tenth, what about all the other big KBOs being discovered? Are all of them planets, too, or just some of them? Which ones exactly? That's when the IAU stepped in, inventing the dwarf planet category and redefining the word *planet.*

Mike Brown told reporters in 2006 that the IAU had done the right thing. "Pluto would never be considered a planet if it were discovered today," he said. In 2008 two more of the big round KBOs that Mike Brown's team discovered, Haumea and Makemake, joined the dwarf-planet club.

Alan Stern disagreed with Pluto's reclassification. "I think the IAU has confused people," he said. He argues that the new definition of *planet* goes against common sense. Wouldn't you call a Pluto-like world a planet if you saw it out of a spaceship window? "Like most planetary scientists I run into, we consider a dwarf planet to be a planet," he said. Dwarf planets are just a smaller variety of planet. "Just as a Chihuahua is still a dog." Alan has never stopped calling Pluto the ninth planet.

Some scientists believe that the IAU may reconsider and reclassify Pluto back to a planet someday. Astronomers are now finding planets orbiting other stars. Many don't easily fit into the planet categories—terrestrial, gas giant, dwarf—that we use for our solar system. The universe is a big place and planets of unimaginable kinds are probably out there! Whether you call it a planet or not, Pluto is a fascinating place. Learn more about icy dwarf planets in the Mission Brief on page 66.

"We're really testing the things we can't simulate on the ground very well," said Alice. Things like slewing, for example. Slewing is moving the spacecraft to aim its cameras and instruments. *New Horizons'* instruments aren't on movable arms. The spacecraft must turn itself to change the instruments' positions. Alice said they needed to make sure there was enough time between slews. There isn't sufficient power for everything to work at once. One set of cameras and science instruments has to be switched off before another set can be turned on.

The spacecraft must also turn away from Pluto and look back toward Earth to receive commands or send back pictures and recorded data. All of this while flying by Pluto at 30,000 miles (48,280 kilometers) per hour. There's a nine-hour delay, remember. So even if pictures of blank sky start showing up in Mission Control, it'll be too late to slow down or move the spacecraft.

"This is a one-chance event," said Alice. It's got to be perfect the first time. "We can't go back." Everything during the Pluto encounter was planned out in advance down to the

WHAT IS A PLANET?

According to the IAU, a space object currently has to pass these three tests to be a planet:

1. **It must orbit the sun. Moons aren't planets, for example, because they orbit another object in space.**

2. **It must be round. Gravity squashes all big space objects—stars, planets, moons—into round balls, or spheres. A sphere is the kind of shape where every part is pulled in as close to the center as possible. If an object isn't massive enough to be a sphere, it isn't a planet.**

3. **It must orbit alone. Those that share their orbits with neighboring objects, such as asteroids or KBOs, aren't planets. They are not massive enough to clear their orbits of other objects. This is the test that Pluto fails.**

millisecond. There are no do-overs, and surprises are unwelcome. The team had backup plans for every imaginable problem. And backup plans for the backup plans, too. Had they thought of everything? "At the top of my worry list," said Alan, "is that we're missing something that we should be worried about."

MULTIPLYING MOONS

Alan Stern had reason to worry about unknowns. His team built *New Horizons* to fly by Pluto and its moon, Charon. They got a surprise in late 2005, after the spacecraft was already at the Florida launch site. New Horizons team members discovered two small moons circling Pluto. Nix and Hydra are small worlds that together could fit inside Rhode Island. But their discovery brought up big questions, such as, What else might be out there? Could it make problems for the mission? Are there even more small moons? Might there be rings around Pluto, too?

"Small moons can give off clouds of dust that spread out to form rings," explained Mark Showalter. Planetary rings aren't solid like a bunch of circling Hula-Hoops. They are bands of orbiting dust, ice, and rock. Mark knows all about planetary rings.

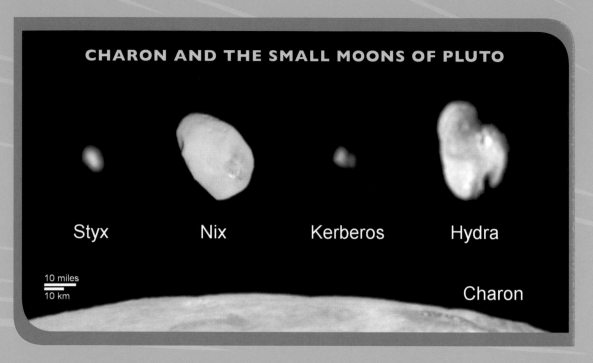

CHARON AND THE SMALL MOONS OF PLUTO

Styx   Nix   Kerberos   Hydra

Charon

10 miles
10 km

"I've spent most of my career studying the ring systems of the four giant planets," he said. Mark discovered one of Jupiter's rings and two rings around Uranus. Moons are another of his specialties. He discovered Saturn's moon Pan, Uranus's moons Mab and Cupid, and the fourteenth moon of Neptune, which isn't named yet.

Mark liked science while growing up. Neil Armstrong's first moonwalk was the most exciting thing he'd ever seen. In high school he mowed lawns to pay for a telescope. *Voyager 1*'s arrival at Jupiter in 1979 turned his interest in astronomy into a career. The space probe's pictures of colorful swirling clouds and giant red storms on our biggest planet fascinated him. When *Voyager 1* moved on to Saturn, its rings captivated him. "They are beautiful," said Mark.

If anyone could find rings around Pluto, Mark Showalter was the one to do it. "I had been using the Hubble telescope to study a lot of other ring systems," recalled Mark. So he focused the Hubble Space Telescope's camera on Pluto and started snapping. No rings showed up, but a white speck of light did. "That little white dot turned out to be Kerberos, Pluto's fourth moon," said Mark. That was the summer of 2011. Mark and his team took another look in 2012. "And that's when Styx turned up," he said.

Pluto has five moons! While studying the new moons, Mark Showalter found that their orbits influence each other and create patterns. "If you're sitting on Nix, Styx goes around twice in one direction every time Hydra goes around three times." That would be something to see.

Finding Kerberos and Styx did more than lengthen the list of Mark's discoveries. "I got added to the New Horizons team because of my Pluto work," he said. Mark is excited about what *New Horizons* discovers. The spacecraft's cameras snapped pictures of all five moons. Did *New Horizons* find more moons, or even rings, circling Pluto? There's no evidence of any so far. Mark and other team members were looking for them, especially as the spacecraft neared Pluto. Surprises can be hazardous.

DODGING DEBRIS

Although amazing, moons and rings are also messy. They create dust and grit that litter space. If the spacecraft hits "anything

MARK SHOWALTER EXPLAINS THAT ALL OF PLUTO'S MOONS ORBIT IN THE SAME DIRECTION AROUND ITS EQUATOR. "THE MOONS FORM A SERIES OF NEATLY NESTED ORBITS, A BIT LIKE RUSSIAN DOLLS," HE SAID.

WHAT'S IN A NAME?

Nix, Hydra, Kerberos, and Styx

Nix is named after the Greek goddess of darkness and night, and Hydra after a terrifying monster with nine heads and a serpent's body. The names were also chosen because their first letters are *N* and *H*, like New Horizons. Members of the New Horizons team discovered them in 2005.

Kerberos is named after the three-headed dog that guards the underworld, and Styx after the Greek goddess of the river with the same name in Pluto's underworld. The names were chosen via a competition and an online vote after Mark Showalter discovered the moons.

SIMILAR LUNAR LEGACY

Where did Pluto's four little moons come from? Were they KBOs captured by Pluto's and Charon's gravity? It doesn't look like it. "We think that they were somehow formed as part of Pluto and Charon," said Mark Showalter. Perhaps a giant *something* slammed into Pluto long ago, knocking off blobs that became moons. "It's probably very similar to how Earth's moon formed." Our moon wasn't there until a Mars-size object collided with a young Earth and created it.

HYDRA

Discovered in: 2005
Distance from Pluto: 40,230 miles (64,740 km)
Size: 27 miles (43 km) at widest point
Days to orbit Pluto: 38

KERBEROS

Discovered in: 2011
Distance from Pluto: 35,910 miles (57,790 km)
Size: 7 1/2 miles (12 km) at widest point
Days to orbit Pluto: 32

NIX

Discovered in: 2005
Distance from Pluto: 30,260 miles (48,700 km)
Size: 33 1/2 miles (54 km) at widest point
Days to orbit Pluto: 25

CHARON

STYX

Discovered in: 2012
Distance from Pluto:
26,510 miles (42,660 km)
Size: 6 miles (10 km) at widest point
Days to orbit Pluto: 20

45

even the size of a rice grain, it could kill us," said Alan Stern. "If it cuts a fuel line, that's bad. If it gets in the main computer and strikes a circuit board, that's not good. It's not good if it knocks out a camera. There's almost no place you want to take a hit."

The odds of something bad happening to *New Horizons* were low. But just in case, the team mapped out alternate routes that would steer the spacecraft into safer space. Those routes, though, wouldn't be as great for pictures. "But better safe than sorry," said Alan. Whether to stay the course or take evasive maneuvers had to be decided sixteen days out from Pluto. What if space pebbles show up after that? Flight controllers can turn *New Horizons* around so it's flying with its dish antenna facing out. That will shield the spacecraft some, though it might mean its cameras aren't facing Pluto. "This may be a bit of a cliffhanger," warned Alan. "Stay tuned."

"I'VE FALLEN IN LOVE WITH THE PLUTO SYSTEM," ADMITS MARK SHOWALTER.
"PLUTO HAS NOT DISAPPOINTED US IN THE PAST; IT'S GIVEN US MANY SURPRISES ALREADY."

Five

UP CLOSE AND PERSONAL

It had already been a very long day. *New Horizons* made its closest flyby of Pluto at 7:50 a.m. on July 14, 2015. Few on the team had slept much the night before, and some not at all. After the morning flyby and its celebration, there were question-and-answer sessions with news reporters and a live broadcast program on NASA Television. Proving the team's motto that "science never sleeps," a few hours later Alice Bowman was back at work in the Mission Operations Center.

No one had heard from *New Horizons* for more than twenty hours. This was as planned. Not talking to Earth allowed the spacecraft to collect the maximum number of close-up pictures, scans, and measurements of Pluto and its moons. With a response time of nine hours, communicating with *New Horizons* wasn't practical. No one yet knew if the spacecraft had passed safely through the Pluto system. Were all the pictures and data successfully recorded? The team was finally about to find out. It was time for *New Horizons* to phone home.

THE SCIENCE TEAM MEMBERS ARE THRILLED BY THEIR FIRST LOOK AT PLUTO.

CHECKING IN FROM PLUTO

In the busy room filled with giant overhead monitors, Alice sat in front of her computer with a headset on, trying not to worry. The MOM watched the minutes on a clock drag by, second by stubborn second. "Stand by for telemetry," she announced over the speaker. The room grew quiet. It was 8:50 p.m., and *New Horizons'* signal was due. Everyone waited, eyes glued to screens, and many held their breath.

At 8:52 p.m. a message came through Alice's headset. "Copy that," she answered. The hint of a smile crossed her face. "We're in lock . . . with the spacecraft," announced Alice. *New Horizons* had called in! It was still out there, but was it OK? Did it record everything? Was the mission a success?

"Subsystems, please report your status," Alice said. One by one, each subsystem engineer reported in. Everything was fine—power, computers, guidance, propulsion—and the memory chips were full of data.

"MOM on Pluto 1," Alice said, standing up. "We have a healthy spacecraft. We've recorded data of the Pluto system and we're outbound from Pluto." Everyone cheered and

clapped, and many jumped out of their seats. Alan Stern stormed through the glass door into the Mission Operations Center. He fist-pumped the air in jubilation and smiled like crazy.

Alan rushed over to Alice and the two hugged. "It's fantastic!" said Alice. Her face beamed with delight. "We did it!"

Alan turned to shake hands with a joyful Chris Hersman. The engineer went right back to clapping after accepting the congratulations, his grin a mile wide. What

FLIGHT CONTROLLERS IN THE MISSIONS OPERATIONS CENTER ARE RELIEVED TO RECEIVE A SIGNAL FROM *NEW HORIZONS* ON THE NIGHT OF JULY 14, 2015.

MISSION BRIEF
Pluto Encounter

WHY JUST FLY BY?

New Horizons is a flyby mission. The spacecraft didn't go into orbit or drop off a lander. Why send just a flyby space probe? Remember that this is the first spacecraft mission to Pluto. It's what space scientists and engineers call a first reconnaissance mission. The first missions to the other planets were also simple, straightforward flybys; nothing too tricky for a first try. Going into orbit around a moon or planet is a complicated maneuver. Braking retrorockets need fuel to slow down the spacecraft so it can enter orbit. It would take a hundred times the amount of fuel that's onboard *New Horizons* to drop into orbit around Pluto. Another reason that New Horizons is a flyby mission is that Pluto wasn't its final destination. The spacecraft is now on its way to Kuiper belt object 2014 MU69.

LAST OF THE FIRSTS

New Horizons will complete NASA's first reconnaissance of the solar system. "The United States was first to every planet," said Alan Stern with pride. Here are the other spacecraft pioneers and the years of their arrivals:

PLANET	MISSION	YEAR
Mercury	Mariner 10	1974
Venus	Mariner 2	1962
Mars	Mariner 4	1965
Jupiter	Pioneer 10	1973
Saturn	Pioneer 11	1979
Uranus	Voyager 2	1986
Neptune	Voyager 2	1989
Pluto	New Horizons	2015

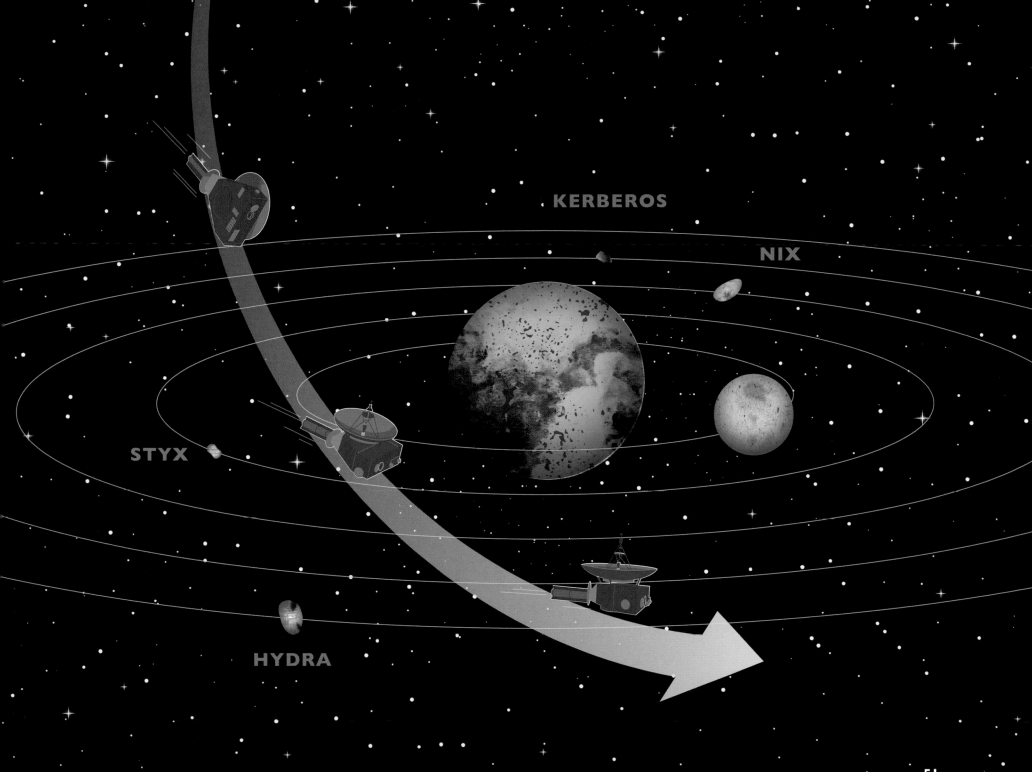

KERBEROS

NIX

STYX

HYDRA

an astounding accomplishment! The team had built a robotic spacecraft packed with cameras and science instruments, flown it across the solar system, and it had perfectly done its job at Pluto. "Just like we planned it," said Alice. "Just like we practiced."

Even the trajectory had cooperated. No new troublesome moons or rings were discovered leading up to the approach. New Horizons scientist John Spencer led the hazard detection team. He would have been excited to find additional moons. "But as a New Horizons team member, I am much more relieved that we didn't find something that could harm the spacecraft." No hazards had to be avoided on approach,

and no debris was encountered. *New Horizons* passed through the Pluto system unharmed.

The team learned that the ten-year-old robotic probe was in fact quite healthy. "Every indication is that the spacecraft is in great shape," said Chris. All of its original parts still worked. Though the team used some of the backup parts at times during the long cruise, said Chris, "we haven't lost anything. No hardware has been lost."

Amazing. Let the discoveries begin!

A SNEAK PEEK

There is so much data onboard *New Horizons,* and its download speed is so slow, that it took sixteen months for all of the data to reach Earth. Only 5 percent of the data came down the week after the flyby in July 2015. Every data packet received so far has delivered astonishing photos and scans full of stunning surprises.

"Home run!" said Alan. "Pluto and Charon are just mind-blowing. *New Horizons* is returning amazing results already." Like

WHAT'S THE BIG DARK AREA AT CHARON'S NORTH POLE? IT COULD BE AN IMPACT CRATER FROM AN ASTEROID OR OTHER KBO SLAMMING INTO IT.

what? How about some basics, such as size. According to new measurements from *New Horizons*, Pluto is 1,473 miles (2,370 kilometers) across. That's about 50 miles (80 kilometers) bigger than was expected. Because scientists had the mass right, being bigger means that Pluto is less dense than they thought. Pluto's insides are likely made up of more ice and less heavy rock. Charon's size remains the same.

"These two objects have been together for billions of years, in the same orbit, but they are totally different," said Alan. They're even different colors. Charon, Pluto's giant moon and binary planet partner, is more gray in color. Pluto is orange-red with darker and lighter areas.

How can an ice-covered world be red? Mars is red from the rusted iron minerals in its soil. Pluto's reddish color comes from something very different. It's a chemical stain on the ice, created by sunlight hitting methane. Also called natural gas, methane is used here on Earth to heat homes and cook food. Pluto has both methane ice on its surface and methane gas in its atmosphere. When ultraviolet light from the sun hits methane gas, it produces gunky red chemicals that rain down on Pluto and stain its surface.

As with a ketchup-spotted shirt, the reddish color isn't evenly spread over Pluto. The dwarf planet's equator area, where more sunlight hits, is the darkest, whereas its north and south poles are lighter. Then there's the huge heart-shaped bright area. Scientists have named Pluto's heart Tombaugh Regio (Tombaugh Region) after Pluto's discoverer. It seems to be a bright, windswept patch of shiny carbon monoxide ice. Where is the frozen carbon monoxide coming from? Why is it just in the heart? These are among the many unanswered questions New Horizons' scientists hope to clear up as more data packets arrive and are studied.

AN ACTIVE WORLD

The entire surface of Pluto has a startling amount of variety. There are mountain ranges, craters, icy plains, and glaciers. New Horizons scientists are already creating maps. They are giving these places names from lists chosen by the public.

There's the impressive Norgay Montes, a mountain

WE "HEART" PLUTO! PLUTO'S BRIGHT HEART-SHAPED REGION WAS NAMED TOMBAUGH REGIO.

range about the height of the Rocky Mountains. The nearby Hillary Montes aren't as high, but the range is longer. These Plutonian mountains aren't rock; they're made of super-hard water ice. Both are in Tombaugh Regio and rise up on the edge of a vast icy plain. Sputnik Planum is the size of Texas. The icy plain is covered in nitrogen ice that moves. Pluto's low temperatures freeze water ice rock-solid. The extreme cold is also why nitrogen, carbon monoxide, and methane can become solid ice, frost, and snow. High-resolution photos of Sputnik Planum from *New Horizons* show ice flowing, similar to glaciers. There are hints of crumbling hillsides, too. That's erosion, another important discovery.

Could it be caused by shifts in the surface? Are there "Pluto-quakes"?

"We've only seen surfaces like this on active worlds like Earth and Mars," said John Spencer. "I'm really smiling." By "active," he means geologically active. Earth's surface is always changing, its features and landscapes constantly re-forming. Mountains get pushed up, canyons are carved out, and lava covers forests. Our planet's geological activity is driven by heat deep inside Earth. A lot of that heat is left over from when Earth was a hot, molten, newborn planet. Some also comes from the decay of radioactive elements in Earth's core. The heat deep inside our planet warms the layer of rock

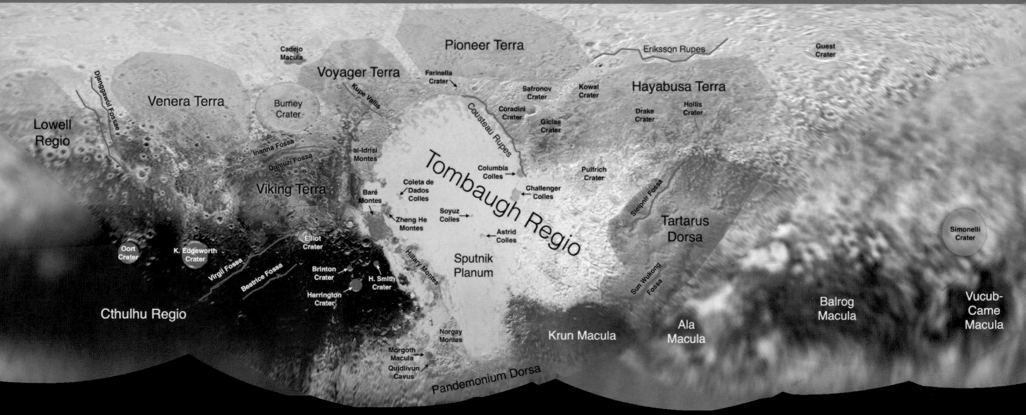

INFORMAL NAMES FOR FEATURES ON PLUTO

Norgay Montes, Sputnik Planum, Vader Crater . . .

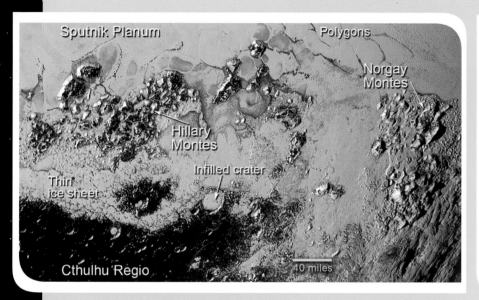

Sputnik Planum

Polygons

Norgay Montes

Hillary Montes

Infilled crater

Thin ice sheet

Cthulhu Regio

40 miles

NORGAY MONTES ARE ABOUT 11,000 FEET (3,500 METERS) HIGH, AND HILLARY MONTES ARE ABOUT HALF THAT HEIGHT.

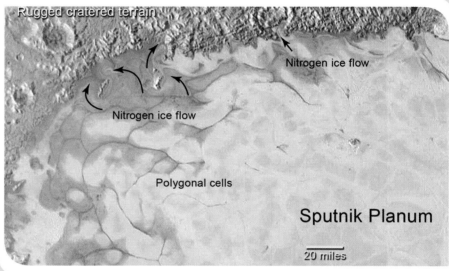

Rugged cratered terrain

Nitrogen ice flow

Nitrogen ice flow

Polygonal cells

Sputnik Planum

20 miles

FLOWING NITROGEN ICE ON SPUTNIK PLANUM LOOKS TO BE ALIEN GLACIERS.

Places and features being discovered on Pluto and its moons need names. In 2015 Mark Showalter organized a campaign to let the public choose names from lists of explorers, writers, and science fiction characters. Hillary Montes and Norgay Montes are named after the first people to summit Mount Everest,

for example. The first artificial Earth satellite, *Sputnik,* and space shuttle *Challenger* are names for plains and hills on Pluto. Charon's features are getting names from the Star Wars, Star Trek, and Dr. Who series, including Spock Crater and Tardis Chasma. None of the names is official yet and some may not stick, but it's a fun start!

on which the continental plates float and move.

In contrast, Mercury is not a geologically active world. Its surface features and landscapes have stayed the same for eons. There are no volcanoes, glaciers, rivers, or earthquakes re-forming it. A crater made a billion years ago remains unchanged on Mercury, the moon, and other "dead," inactive worlds. Not so on active Pluto; its craters are probably erased over time.

Much of Pluto's surface has recently changed. Some areas are only tens of millions of years old or younger. That's a blink of an eye for planetary scientists. Small worlds aren't supposed to be active. They cool more quickly than large planets, like hot french fries compared with a whole baked potato. It's true that some moons are active, such as Jupiter's Io and Saturn's Enceladus. Their heat comes from being pulled and pushed around by their big planet, however. This isn't happening on Pluto. "There's something very different about Plutonian geology," said John.

What makes Pluto geologically active? John said that they knew Pluto has some internal heating from uranium and other radioactive elements. But enough to build mountains and re-form the surface? That was the big surprise delivered by New Horizons. Perhaps a surface of nitrogen, carbon monoxide, and methane ice is more changeable than one of water ice. "This may cause us to rethink what powers geological activity on many other icy worlds," said John. Scientists can't assume anymore that all small, distant, icy places are dead worlds. "Finding that Pluto is geologically active after 4.5 billion years—there's not big enough typeface to write that [headline] in," said Alan. "It's unbelievable."

FRAN BAGENAL EXPLAINS WHAT THEY'VE LEARNED SO FAR ABOUT PLUTO FROM THE MISSION.

AMAZING ATMOSPHERE

Pluto's surprises don't stop at its surface. Like Earth's, Pluto's atmosphere is made mostly of nitrogen. The blanket of air around Pluto reaches much higher than ours, compared with the planet's size. Scientists were dumbfounded to find out that it goes 1,000 miles (1,600 kilometers) above the surface of the planet. That's more than double the height they expected. The spacecraft measured a huge amount of nitrogen gas escaping from Pluto's thin air into space—around five hundred tons every hour. How is Pluto able to constantly replenish its atmosphere? Where's all this new nitrogen coming from? Add those questions to the list of unknowns for now.

The thinner a planet's air, the less weather there is. Tornadoes and heat waves don't happen on the moon, for example. Finding significant weather in Pluto's thin atmosphere is another *New Horizons* discovery. There is definitely haze, and wind probably plays a part in the drifting ice or snow found on Sputnik Planum. Snow falls on Pluto, too, though Fran joked that you wouldn't want to ski on Norgay Montes. "The snow is probably too compact and too hard," she said.

Pluto also has a sort of tail, not unlike a comet's. The PEPSSI and SWAP instruments detected it during flyby. It's created by the solar wind as it carries away charged particles from Pluto's atmosphere. "We have actually flown through this tail," said Fran. "This is just a first tantalizing look." There's a lot more to come.

Alan agrees. "Pluto has a very complicated story to tell," he said. "There is a lot of work we need to do to understand this very complicated place." You won't catch anyone on the New Horizons team complaining about that. Mark Showalter,

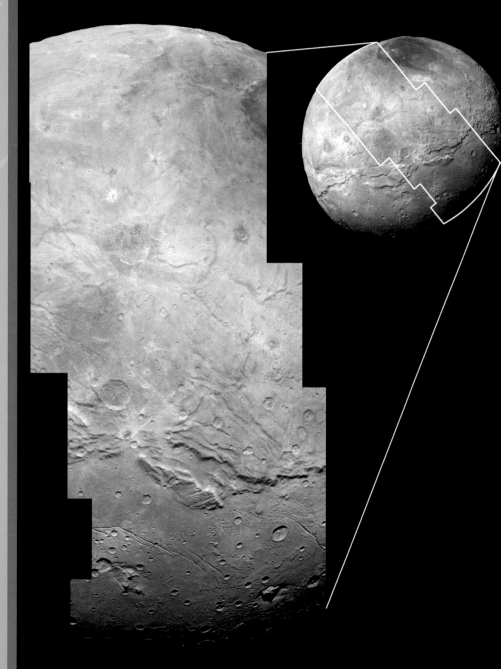

THIS ENHANCED COLOR IMAGE OF CHARON FROM *NEW HORIZONS* HIGHLIGHTS ITS HUGE CANYON, MANY CRATERS, AND ODD DARK POLE, MORDOR MACULA.

New Horizons' Discoveries So Far

SOME OF THE SUPER-CLOSE-UP IMAGES OF PLUTO SHOW UNEXPLAINABLY COMPLEX LANDSCAPES, INCLUDING THIS "SNAKESKIN" ONE. "IT'S REALLY COMPLICATED," SAID ALAN ABOUT HIS FAVORITE PLANET. "THIS IS GOING TO BE A VERY TOUGH STORY TO UNRAVEL."

Scientists are studying the pictures and information received from *New Horizons*, and will continue to make discoveries in the coming years. "We've turned a new page in the study of Pluto," said Alan Stern. "I wish Pluto's discoverer, Clyde Tombaugh, had lived to see this day." These were some of the mission's major discoveries as of May 2016 (when this book went to press):

- Pluto is about 50 miles (80 kilometers) larger than expected.

- Pluto's surface isn't all the same. There are tall water-ice mountains like Norgay Montes, glaciers, and icy, craterless plains divided into strange cell-shaped patterns.

- Pluto isn't a dead world. It's geologically active and at least some of its surface has changed recently. There might even be ice volcanos!

- The atmosphere around Pluto is about twice as big as scientists thought. It extends about 1,000 miles (1,600 kilometers) above the surface and includes blue haze.

- Charon's surface has a variety of features. It has an enormous canyon system, a dark reddish pole, and a mountain in a moat.

- The four minimoons of the Pluto system are quite different from each other. Nix and Hydra have very bright white surfaces for their age, possibly from ice.

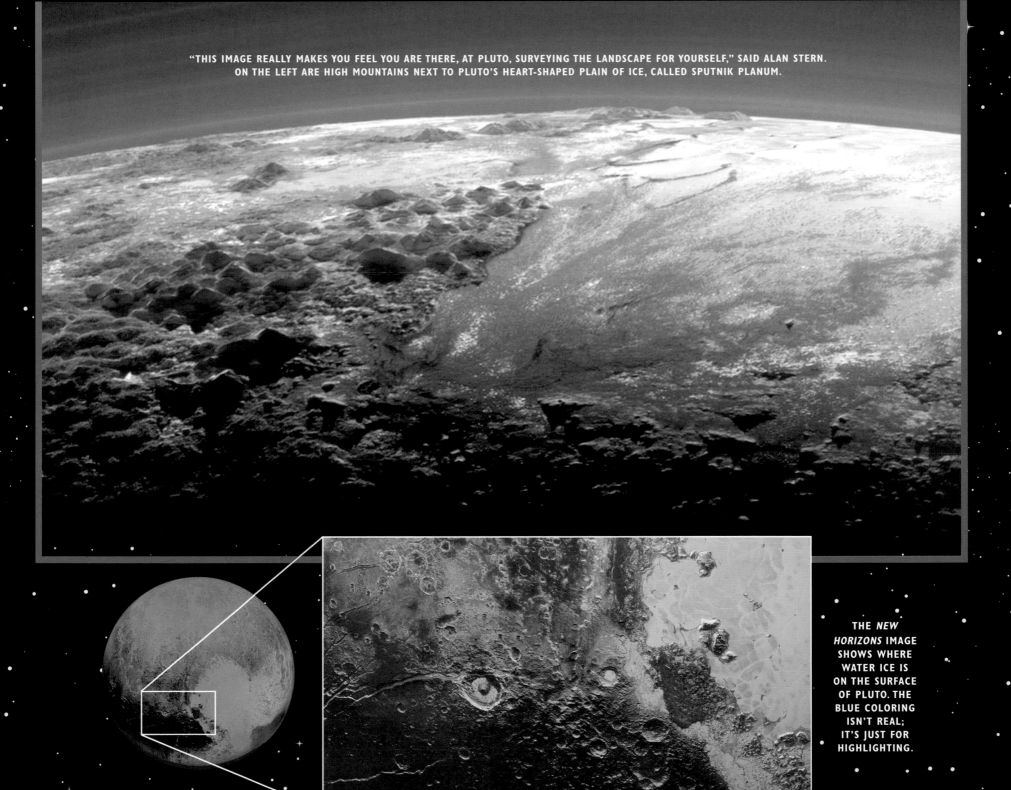

"THIS IMAGE REALLY MAKES YOU FEEL YOU ARE THERE, AT PLUTO, SURVEYING THE LANDSCAPE FOR YOURSELF," SAID ALAN STERN. ON THE LEFT ARE HIGH MOUNTAINS NEXT TO PLUTO'S HEART-SHAPED PLAIN OF ICE, CALLED SPUTNIK PLANUM.

THE *NEW HORIZONS* IMAGE SHOWS WHERE WATER ICE IS ON THE SURFACE OF PLUTO. THE BLUE COLORING ISN'T REAL; IT'S JUST FOR HIGHLIGHTING.

59

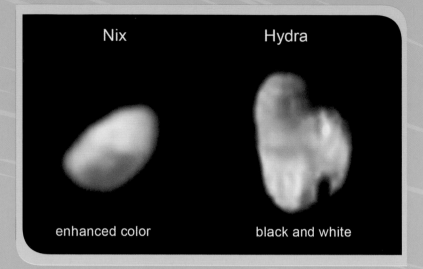

Nix   Hydra

enhanced color   black and white

**NEW HORIZONS SNAPPED SOME CLOSE-UPS OF
MINIATURE MOONS NIX AND HYDRA.**

the moon and ring guy, said that the Pluto flyby is the most exciting thing he's ever been involved in. "Pluto has not disappointed us one bit," he said. "It is an utterly fascinating world."

ICY SYSTEM

The five moons of Pluto didn't disappoint either. "It's a mini solar system," said Mark. Charon was full of surprises. The gray matriarch of Pluto's moons turns out to have some recently active regions, too. It's not a geologically dead moon. There's a thousand-mile-long canyon that's twice as deep as the Grand Canyon in places. "It looks like the entire crust of Charon has been split open," said John Spencer. Charon also has cliffs and troughs, and a big, mysterious dark spot at its north pole. What really stunned and stumped scientists was what appeared to be a large mountain sitting in a moat!

New Horizons also photographed and scanned Pluto's four small moons. Early findings reveal Hydra as a mitten-shaped

world covered in water ice and about 27 miles (43 kilometers) across. The simultaneously discovered, similarly sized Nix is more jellybean-shaped. Both seem to have craters. Pluto's minimoon Kerberos is different from the others, said Mark. It looks dark and very dense. "Sort of like a charcoal briquette," he said. And the tiniest moon, Styx, turns out to be oblong, nearly twice as long as it is wide. With more pictures and measurements, he hopes to learn how all six members of the Pluto system became a family.

We already have the last picture that *New Horizons* took of Pluto. After passing through the system on July 14, 2015, the spacecraft looked back and snapped a photo of Pluto's silhouette. Backlit by the sun, the icy dwarf's atmosphere is a blue, hazy, glowing crown. "My jaw was on the ground when I saw this," said Alan. Our own familiar sun illuminating an alien atmosphere in the distant Kuiper belt. "It reminds us that exploration brings us more than just incredible discoveries—it brings incredible beauty."

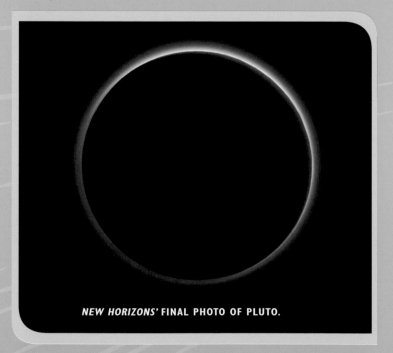

NEW HORIZONS' FINAL PHOTO OF PLUTO.

MEET THE NEIGHBORS

What's next for *New Horizons*? "We're going exploring into the Kuiper belt," said Alan. Pluto is just "the first discovered, the biggest, and the brightest of a whole population of small planets that orbit within the Kuiper belt." The Kuiper belt is like a dark, icy, supersize asteroid belt. The first Kuiper belt object (KBO) was discovered in 1992. "Today, more than sixteen hundred are known," said Alan. KBOs come in a variety of colors and shapes. Some are circled by tiny moons, but not all. Ices cover their surfaces, but most have no atmosphere.

"We didn't know it until recently," said Alan, "but our solar system—and probably others—was very good at making small planets." Dwarf planets aren't oddballs; they're a very common kind of world. "It's not the terrestrials that are normal, it's not the [gas] giant planets that are normal, it's the little ones." Alan said this shift in thinking is a revolution in planetary

then. The leftovers from the planet-making process have not. Solar system scraps such as comets, asteroids, and KBOs are like fossils, or bits of ancient history. "There's a real record of the early history of the solar system out there in cold storage, beyond Neptune," said New Horizons scientist John Spencer. It was his job to find a KBO for *New Horizons* to visit.

HUNTING FOR KBOs

New Horizons was built to go farther than Pluto, billions of miles farther. Onboard is extra fuel to steer it toward a KBO. The spacecraft's instruments can work in light dimmer than at Pluto and still be able to communicate with Earth. This was all figured out before the launch in 2006. What wasn't worked out was where it would go. Smaller KBOs are the true frozen, unchanged leftovers from the formation of the solar system. So the goal was to find one KBO between 12 and 31 miles (20–50 kilometers) wide that *New Horizons* could go to after Pluto. The team had until the flyby in 2015 to find it. How hard could it be?

John Spencer was determined to make it happen. "This is the one chance in my lifetime that we're going to get a spacecraft out there and look up close at one of these Kuiper belt objects." John has been on the Pluto mission team for twenty-three years. The planetary astronomer and native Brit is used to keeping calm and taking on the mission's ever-changing challenges. John was also the hazard *jefe,* the guy making sure *New Horizons'* flyby path was safe and debris-free.

John Spencer's Pluto connections run deep, all the way back to its discoverer. John used to work at the same observatory in Arizona as Clyde Tombaugh. "In fact, I lived in a house

science. In fact, he said, "it may be that the dwarf planets are not only the most common kind of planet in the solar system, they *may* be the most common abode for life in the solar system." Scientists think some icy dwarfs have oceans below their surfaces. Liquid water is necessary to run the chemistry of life as we know it. KBOs, including Pluto, have organics. Organics are materials containing the element carbon and make up the building blocks of life. Everything from tree bark to bacteria is made of organics. Methane and the red-brown chemicals that stain Pluto's ice are organics because both contain carbon.

KBOs also hold clues to how our solar system came to be and why it looks the way it does. Planets formed as debris from the sun's starry birth clumped together, grew into spheres, then heated and cooled. Planets like Earth have changed a lot since

THE KBO THAT *NEW HORIZONS* WILL STUDY IS PROBABLY SIMILAR TO THE SMALL, ICY CHUNK OF HISTORY ILLUSTRATED HERE.

JOHN SPENCER HAS A BACKGROUND IN GEOLOGY. "BUT I'VE BECOME MORE OF AN ASTRONOMER AS MY CAREER HAS PROGRESSED," HE SAID. "I DO QUITE A LOT OF DIFFERENT THINGS." BESIDES PLUTO AND ITS MOONS, JOHN HAS STUDIED VOLCANOES ON JUPITER'S MOON IO AND ICE ERUPTIONS ON SATURN'S MOON ENCELADUS.

that was on the same site where he had lived when he worked at Lowell Observatory," said John. "That was cool; the office where he discovered Pluto was only twenty yards away."

John remembers when he realized the search for a KBO was going to be tough. It was years before *New Horizons'* launch. He was on an airplane chatting with another team member. That's when John had an "uh-oh" moment. He recalled thinking, "The place we have to look is going to be right in the Milky Way." Searching for faint objects in the part of the sky where the Milky Way glows in the background is hard to do. It's like picking out a birthday candle's flame in front of a bonfire.

But the KBO search team had no choice. "It's just a tiny sliver of the Kuiper belt that we can actually get to," said John. *New Horizons* has limited fuel for changing course. At the time, there were no known small KBOs in the section reachable by the spacecraft, though no one had actually looked. "Who in their right mind would try looking for KBOs in the Milky Way if they didn't have to?" said John. But other sections of the Kuiper belt did have enough KBOs of the right size. "Our thinking was, 'There are probably some in that little sliver, too,'" he said. "Then we had to go find them."

FROM THE GROUND UP

Astronomers put the world's most powerful telescopes to

63

AN ARTIST'S IDEA OF WHAT *NEW HORIZONS'* VISIT TO A KBO MIGHT LOOK LIKE.

work in the hunt for a KBO. They scanned the night skies from mountaintop observatories in Chile and Hawaii. "We did three years of searching, and we found a whole bunch of KBOs," said John. "But none of them were close enough to the spacecraft's trajectory."

The situation looked grim in 2014, just a year out from the Pluto encounter. The search team had only a few months left to look. If they didn't find possible KBOs soon, there wouldn't be time to track the KBOs' orbits, map out trajectories, and plan a route for the spacecraft. "We are running out of time," said Alan in 2014. *New Horizons'* cruise through the

Kuiper belt might be a lonely one.

"We started to get worried that we could not find anything suitable," said John. "That's when we turned to the Hubble." The Hubble Space Telescope orbits above Earth's blurring atmosphere. Perhaps its super-sharp vision would pick out KBOs that the spacecraft could reach. Getting to use the Hubble isn't easy; a long line of scientists want to do the same. But the KBO search team was able to get a bit of observation time. Once pictures started coming back from the Hubble, John and his team scoured them for faint moving objects that could be KBOs. Each picture had a million stars in it that are brighter than the KBOs. John's team wrote special software so that computers could help search the Hubble images.

"In the end, the space telescope came to the rescue," said John. "It was a real thrill when we found that first object." The bigger thrill came months later, once the team had tracked the orbit of the KBO and knew the spacecraft could reach it. "Those were really exciting moments," recalled John. "We had actually succeeded in this crazy thing!" *New Horizons* was headed for a piece of the solar system's ancient past. After a ten-year search, Alan Stern could finally announce, "We have a KBO to fly by." Its name, at least for now, is 2014 MU69.

What's the KBO like? To begin with, 2014 MU69 is just under 30 miles (45 kilometers) wide, or ten times the size of

a comet. It's a hundred thousand times fainter than Pluto. What will the spacecraft show us about the KBO? Its shape and the kinds of rocks and ices it's made of, for starters. "Whether it has moons will be very interesting to see," said John. "We might see where something has collided with it and made a crater that splashed fresh material onto the surface." That could tell us what's down underneath. The only sure thing is that KBO 2014 MU69 will look different from Pluto.

New Horizons won't get to the KBO for a while. "We have the distance to cross the Kuiper belt, about one-third as great as the distance we flew to get to Pluto—another billion miles," said Alan. "So it's quite a journey." Estimated time of arrival? Early 2019. In the meantime, scientists around the world will

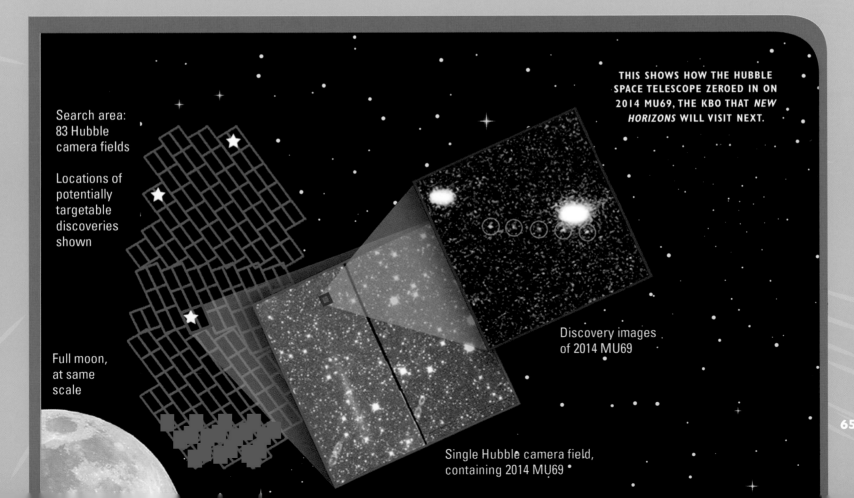

Search area: 83 Hubble camera fields

Locations of potentially targetable discoveries shown

Full moon, at same scale

THIS SHOWS HOW THE HUBBLE SPACE TELESCOPE ZEROED IN ON 2014 MU69, THE KBO THAT *NEW HORIZONS* WILL VISIT NEXT.

Discovery images of 2014 MU69

Single Hubble camera field, containing 2014 MU69

MISSION BRIEF
The Kuiper Belt

WHAT'S IN A NAME?

Kuiper Belt

Gerard Kuiper is often called the father of planetary science. In the 1950s he wrote about the possibility of a ring of small objects beyond Neptune. No telescope at the time was powerful enough to see if he was right. After actual objects were found, astronomers named the Kuiper belt in his honor.

KUIPER BELT FACTS

- It is a band of rocky and icy objects past Neptune.

- In 1992 scientists using telescopes found the very first Kuiper belt object.

- The Kuiper belt is often called the third zone of the solar system. The first zone consists of the rocky planets, and the second zone is where the gas giants orbit.

- The Kuiper belt is similar to the asteroid belt between Mars and Jupiter, but asteroids are more rocky and KBOs more icy.

- It is the largest region in the solar system.

- The Kuiper belt holds an estimated 100,000-plus miniature worlds with diameters larger than 100 kilometers.

It may be the most famous icy dwarf planet, but Pluto isn't the only one. So far three other KBO worlds have joined its ranks—massive Eris, reddish Makemake, and egg-shaped Haumea. What KBO will next be named a dwarf planet?

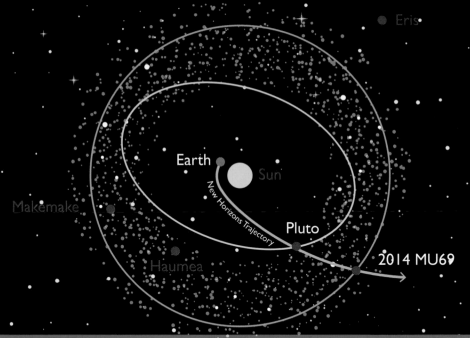

Earth

Sun

New Horizons Trajectory

Eris

Makemake

Haumea

Pluto

2014 MU69

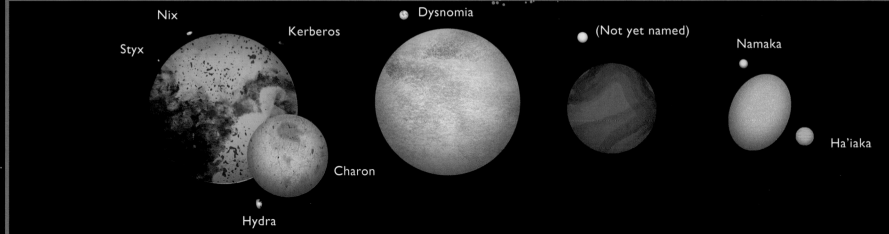

Nix

Styx

Kerberos

Dysnomia

(Not yet named)

Namaka

Charon

Ha'iaka

Hydra

	PLUTO	ERIS	MAKEMAKE	HAUMEA
Discovered:	1930	2005	2005	2004
Distance from sun compared to Earth's distance:	39 1/2 times as far	68	46	43
Size in diameter:	1,473 miles (2,370 km)	1,445 miles (2,326 km)	889 miles (1,430 km)	777 miles (1,250 km)
Length of year:	248 Earth years	558 Earth years	309 Earth years	284 Earth years
Known moons:	5	1	1	2

keep studying all the new information about the Pluto system that *New Horizons* sent back. Understanding what it all means will take decades. Pluto will probably hold on to a few of its secrets a while longer.

New Horizons' journey won't end with the KBO flyby. The spacecraft will soldier on, eventually passing through the Kuiper belt and into deep space. We'll keep hearing from it until its RTG runs out of plutonium. After that, *New Horizons* won't be able to power the transmitter. When will that happen? "We've estimated that will be in the mid- to late 2030s, around the year 2035," said Alan. "By that time the spacecraft will be almost three times as far as Pluto is from the sun." That's almost as far as the twin *Voyager* spacecrafts are now.

Voyager 1 and *2* left Earth nearly forty years ago. They were built in the 1970s. *New Horizons'* technology is more advanced than what's on the *Voyagers*, said Alan. "We have a great suite of instrumentation to study the border with interstellar space." Alan never gets tired of wondering about what's farther out there. He believes that the desire and drive to explore are part of who we are as human beings. Who knows what else *New Horizons* will discover on the very edge of the solar system? So stay tuned, said Alan. "*New Horizons* could go on for another twenty-five or so years."

NEW HORIZONS MISSION LEADER ALAN STERN.

Words to Know

ANTENNA: A rod, wire, or metal dish that sends and/or receives radio waves.

ASTEROID: A rocky space object measuring from a few hundred feet to several hundred miles in diameter that orbits the sun.

ASTEROID BELT: The region of space between Mars and Jupiter where most asteroids are found.

ASTRONOMER: A scientist who studies stars, planets, and other space objects.

ASTRONOMY: The study of moons, stars, planets, and everything else in space.

ATMOSPHERE: The layer of gases that surrounds a planet, moon, or other object in space and that is kept from escaping by the object's gravity.

ATMOSPHERIC PRESSURE: Measure of the force exerted on a surface by the weight of the air above it.

BINARY PLANET: Two worlds that orbit a combined center of mass that lies outside both objects.

CARBON DIOXIDE: A colorless gas made of a combination of carbon and twice the number of oxygen atoms; CO_2.

CARBON MONOXIDE: A colorless gas made of an equal combination of carbon and oxygen atoms; CO.

CHARGED PARTICLES: Tiny bits of matter with electrical charges, including electrons, protons, and ions.

CHASMA: A long, deep, steep depression on a planet or moon.

COMET: A space object made of dust, frozen water, and gases that orbits the sun.

CRATERS: Bowl-shaped depressions made by impact explosions, often by comet or asteroid crashes.

DAY: The time it takes an object in space to complete one rotation, or spin.

DWARF PLANET: A round space object that orbits the sun and may orbit with other objects.

ELECTROMAGNETIC (EM) SPECTRUM: The entire range of electromagnetic radiation types.

FLYBY PROBE: A space probe that flies by a planet or moon.

GAS GIANT: A planet made mostly of gas and liquid and no land; Jupiter, Saturn, Uranus, and Neptune are gas giants.

GEOLOGY: The study of rocks, soils, and minerals.

GLACIER: A mass of moving ice.

ICE DWARF: An ice-covered space object larger than a comet that orbits beyond Neptune.

INFRARED LIGHT: Invisible electromagnetic radiation that has a long wavelength and that is experienced as heat.

KUIPER BELT: A region containing millions of chunks and spheres of ice and rock beyond Neptune.

KUIPER BELT OBJECT, OR KBO: An icy space object in the Kuiper belt.

LANDER: A space probe that sets down on the surface of a planet or other object in space.

MACULA: A dark area on the surface of a planet or moon.

MAGNETIC FIELD: The area of magnetic influence around a magnet, electric current, or planet.

MAGNETOSPHERE: The region of space influenced by the magnetic field of a planet or moon.

METHANE: Natural gas, or a gas made from a combination of carbon and hydrogen; CH_4.

MICROMETEORITES: Tiny rocks in space.

MILKY WAY: The galaxy to which the sun, our solar system, and all the visible stars in the night sky belong.

MONTES: A mountain range on a planet or moon.

MOON: An object in space that naturally orbits a larger object in space.

NASA: The National Aeronautics and Space Administration; the U.S. space agency.

NITROGEN: A common gas; N_2.

ORBIT: The looping or circling path followed by a planet, moon, or other object in space around another object; to move around an object.

ORBITER: A space probe that orbits a planet, moon, or other object in space.

ORGANICS: Chemicals with carbon that can be the building blocks of living, or once living, things.

PAYLOAD: Cargo or instruments carried by a spacecraft.

PLANET: A round space object that orbits the sun and is alone in its orbit.

PLANETARY ASTRONOMER: An astronomer who studies planets and moons.

PLANUM: A high plain or plateau on a planet or moon.

PLASMA: Very hot gases that are good conductors of electricity and are affected by a magnetic field.

PLUTONIUM: A radioactive element usually produced from uranium and discovered in the 1940s.

PROPELLANT: The fuel for a rocket engine.

RADIATION: Electromagnetic energy such as gamma rays, x-rays, ultraviolet light, visible light, infrared radiation, microwaves, and radio waves.

RADIOACTIVE: A substance that produces a powerful form of radiation energy.

RADIO WAVES: A type of electromagnetic radiation that has the lowest frequency and the longest wavelength.

REGIO: A region or large area with a distinctive color or brightness.

RING: A thin band of dust, rocks, and ice particles orbiting a planet.

RTG: A radioisotope thermoelectric generator; a plutonium power source of electricity for spacecraft.

SLEWING: Turning or sliding in another direction very quickly.

SOLAR SYSTEM: The sun and everything that orbits it.

SOLAR WIND: The constant stream of charged particles given off by the sun.

SPACE PROBE: A robotic spacecraft sent into space to collect information.

SPACE SHUTTLE: One of NASA's Space Transportation System vehicles that launched into the Earth's orbit with astronauts and equipment onboard and later landed on a runway.

SPACE TELESCOPE: A telescope that orbits Earth or travels in space.

SPECTROMETER: An instrument that measures and/or maps wavelengths of light, or both.

TELEMETRY: Information and measurements sent by radio.

TERRESTRIAL PLANET: A rocky solid planet with a metal center; Mercury, Venus, Earth, and Mars are terrestrial planets.

THRUSTER: A small rocket attached to a spacecraft that controls its position.

TRAJECTORY: The path a space object or spacecraft travels through space.

ULTRAVIOLET LIGHT: Invisible electromagnetic radiation that has a very short wavelength.

URANIUM: A radioactive metal element.

VACUUM: Space that is empty of matter.

VISIBLE LIGHT: Electromagnetic radiation that human eyes can see.

WAVELENGTH: The distance between two adjacent peaks of a wave of light, sound, or other energy.

X-RAY: Penetrating electromagnetic radiation with an extremely short wavelength.

YEAR: The time it takes for an object in space to travel around the sun.

Find Out More

NEW HORIZONS

The best way to find out where the spacecraft is now and what fascinating findings are being made is to go online and to social media.

- New Horizons: pluto.jhuapl.edu

  This official website features a map showing where the spacecraft is at the moment and how long and how far it's traveled. The home page has links to the latest news, photos, and everything you'd ever want to know about Pluto and the mission. Plus you can subscribe to eNews so that updates will be emailed directly to you. Get clicking!

- Facebook: www.facebook.com/new.horizons1

- Twitter: @NASANewHorizons

- YouTube: www.youtube.com/user/ NASANewHorizons

PLUTO, ICY DWARF PLANETS, AND THE KUIPER BELT WEBSITES

- Pluto 101: pluto.jhuapl.edu/Participate/learn/ What-We-Know.php

- "What Is Pluto?": www.nasa.gov/audience/ forstudents/5-8/features/nasa-knows/what- is-pluto-58.html

- "Solar System Exploration": solarsystem.nasa. gov/planets/ (click on "Dwarf Planets" or "Kuiper Belt")

AUTHOR'S NOTE OF THANKS

The idea for this book began more than a decade ago. As someone who has written about the solar system for many years (and is a certified space geek), I followed the news accounts of *New Horizons'* 2006 launch. As the years passed, while *New Horizons* was on its way to Pluto, I talked about the spacecraft with students during school visits. "It'll be there in nine years," I said early on. Then it was "in seven years; . . . in five years; . . . in three years. . . ." I remember when it finally became "next year!" and I realized that the people and spacecraft involved in such an epic journey deserved to have their story told.

This book about the New Horizons mission would not have been possible without the hundreds of engineers and scientists who designed, built, and flew the spacecraft across the solar system. Thank you for all your hard work, creative thinking, and perseverance. Congratulations on your success. You all rock! It's a monumental achievement.

First and foremost among those we'd like to thank is New Horizons' principal investigator, S. Alan Stern, of the Southwest Research Institute. The human race owes him a thank-you card. To his further credit, it was Alan Stern's idea to make this book about the entire New Horizons team. It's richer because of it. Our gratitude goes out to those team members, chief among them Alice Bowman and Chris Hersman of the Applied Physics Laboratory (APL) at The Johns Hopkins University. Science team members John Spencer of the Southwest Research Institute, Fran Bagenal of the University of Colorado, and Mark Showalter of the SETI (Search for Extraterrestial Intelligence) Institute provided invaluable assistance by agreeing to interviews and photo shoots as well. We would also like to express our gratitude for the support of APL public information officer Mike Buckley. Attending the flyby events at APL was a once-in-a-lifetime experience! A shout-out is owed to our ever-faithful dog sitters, Tonya and David Herron, and Ann Uhlman and Mark Kater. And last but by no means least, we're ever indebted to our editor, Erica Zappy Wainer, for making us a veteran Scientists in the Field team. Thanks, everyone!

—Mary Kay and Tom

Sources & Selected Bibliography

The quotations by New Horizons team members Alan Stern, Alice Bowman, Chris Hersman, Fran Bagenal, John Spencer, and Mark Showalter were obtained primarily in person and via telephone interviews with the author, as well as from press conferences that the author attended the week of the flyby in July 2015, and official NASA and the Johns Hopkins University Applied Physics Laboratory (JHU/APL) press releases. Every quoted member of the New Horizons team has reviewed his or her quotes in the book. Other significant sources, including those for historical quotes, are the following:

Boyle, Alan. *The Case for Pluto.* 2010. Hoboken, N.J.: John Wiley.

Brown, Mike. *How I Killed Pluto.* 2010. New York: Spiegel & Grau.

Erickson, Jim. "High Winds Delay Launch of Pluto Probe." *Rocky Mountain News,* January 18, 2006.

Haag, Amanda. "A Man with a Mission." *Nature* 436 (August 2005).

Haines-Stiles, Geoffrey. *The Year of Pluto.* NASA. June 12, 2015. www.youtube.com/watch?v=xzae4kKEZV4.

Jones, Barrie W. *Pluto: Sentinel of the Outer Solar System.* 2010. Cambridge: Cambridge University Press.

Levy, David H. *Clyde Tombaugh: Discoverer of the Planet Pluto.* 1991. Tucson: University of Arizona Press.

Mann, Adam. "Get Ready to Learn a Bunch of Awesome New Science About Pluto." *Wired,* September 30, 2014.

"Pluto Demoted, Caltech Scientist Gets 'Dwarf Planet.'" *Pasadena (Calif.) Star News,* August 24, 2006.

Randall, Terri, dir. "Chasing Pluto." *Nova.* Boston, WGBH-TV, July 15, 2015.

Seguela, Philippe. *Space Probes: 50 Years of Exploration from Luna 1 to New Horizons.* 2011. Richmond Hill, Ont.: Firefly Books.

Stern, S. Alan. "Exploring Pluto and Its Satellites at the Solar System's Frontier: New Horizons, One Year and Counting." Smithsonian National Air and Space Museum. Washington, D.C. July 16, 2014. www.ustream.tv/recorded/50177762

———. "KBO Hunting: How Hubble Rescued New Horizons. PI Perspective." September 23, 2014. nasa.gov/directorates/heo/reports/iss-reports/09132012.html

———. *Our Worlds: The Magnetism and Thrill of Planetary Exploration.* 1999. Cambridge: Cambridge University Press.

———. *Worlds Beyond: The Thrill of Planetary Exploration.* 2002. Cambridge: Cambridge University Press.

Stern, S. Alan, and Jacqueline Mitton. *Pluto and Charon: Ice Worlds on the Ragged Edge of the Solar System.* 2009. New York: John Wiley and Sons.

Szalay, J. R., M. Piquette, and M. Horanyi. "The Student Dust Counter: Status report at 23 AU." *Earth Planets Space* 65, no.10 (2013): 1145.

Photo Credits

Index

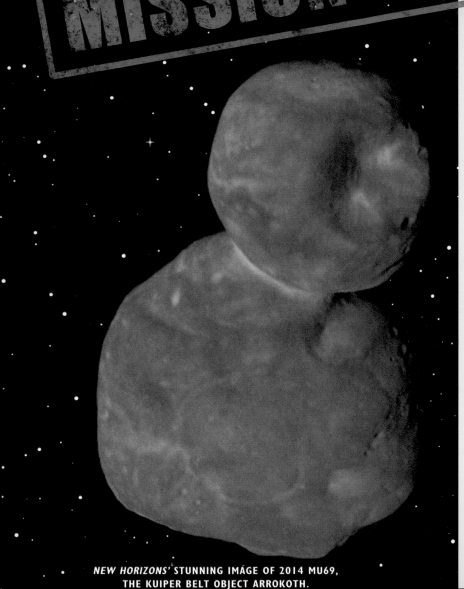

NEW HORIZONS' STUNNING IMAGE OF 2014 MU69, THE KUIPER BELT OBJECT ARROKOTH.

New Horizons makes history again! On January 1, 2019, the spacecraft made a perfect flyby of Kuiper belt object 2014 MU69, now officially named Arrokoth. (The name means "sky" in the Native American Powhatan/Algonquian language.) *New Horizons* flew 2,200 miles (3,500 kilometers) from Arrokoth's surface when the KBO was about 4.1 billion miles (6.6 billion kilometers) from the sun. This makes it the most distant flyby ever—and an astonishing accomplishment. "No other mission has ever targeted and explored an object that hadn't even been discovered when it launched," said Alan Stern.

If that wasn't amazing enough, scientists around the world were stunned when images of Arrokoth came in. The 22-mile-long (35-kilometer-long) KBO isn't a single object; it's two rounded lobes. And they're stuck together—kind of like a rust-colored snowman! Nothing like it has ever been seen anywhere in the solar system. Scientists think that Arrokoth's two lobes once orbited each other as binary worlds, not unlike Pluto and Charon do today. Something happened long ago that caused them to merge. Billions of years ago when the solar system was forming, lots of bits and pieces crashed and clumped together. It's how the planets were made. Arrokoth is like a snapshot of that process frozen in time.

What's next for *New Horizons*? As of July 2019, the spacecraft is healthy and continuing its journey through the Kuiper belt. Its long-range camera is checking out distant KBOs, and other instruments continue to map space plasma and measure solar wind. Will it reach interstellar space someday? It just might—so stay tuned!